MAKING
FRIENDS
WITH YOUR
MOTHER

Other books by Kay Marshall Strom

Chosen Families: Is Adoption for You?
Helping Women in Crisis
Perfect in His Eyes: Studies on Self-Esteem

MAKING FRIENDS WITH YOUR MOTHER

A BOOK FOR DAUGHTERS

Kay Marshall Strom

ZondervanPublishingHouse

Grand Rapids, Michigan

A Division of HarperCollinsPublishers

Making Friends with Your Mother
Copyright © 1991 by Kay Marshall Strom

Requests for information should be addressed to:
Zondervan Publishing House
1415 Lake Drive S.E.
Grand Rapids, Michigan 49506

Library of Congress Cataloging-in-Publication Data

Strom, Kay Marshall, 1943–
    Making friends with your mother / Kay Marshall Strom.
      p. cm.
    ISBN 0-310-53251-5
    1. Mothers and daughters—United States. 2. Motherhood—
Religious aspects—Christianity. I. Title.
HQ759.S815 1991
306.874′3—dc20   90–47254
                                                    CIP

Edited by Linda Vanderzalm

Printed in the United States of America

91 92 93 94 95 / PP / 10 9 8 7 6 5 4 3 2 1

This book is lovingly dedicated to
my mother, Marjorie Marshall,
who made it all possible, and
my daughter, Lisa,
who made it all worthwhile.

CONTENTS

Introduction

Making friends with your mother. What an interesting idea! But is it really possible? Even after all the two of you have said to each other? Even after all the bitterness and animosity that has built up between you? Even with *your* mother?

Yes, even with all that, friendship with your mother really is possible. It may take time. It probably will take effort. And it certainly will take patience. But it can be done. And if you are willing to invest the time, effort, and patience necessary, you are sure to find that the results are well worth the investment.

Because each of us has a different background, because so many variables have worked together to shape us into the person each of us has become, and because our mothers are as diverse and unique as we are, the situations each of us deals with will differ greatly.

Some of the situations are new to the age in which we live—an aging society, mothers divorced after decades of marriage, a vastly differing lifestyle between mother and daughter. Others are, as my grandmother used to say, "as old as the hills"—the struggle to declare your independence from your mother, the struggle to break free from negative traits you learned at your mother's knee.

Some of the situations with which you will need to cope have been popping up in our families for generations— feuds and bitterness and manipulation and a cold distancing of a mother from her children. Isn't it time to lay these legacies to rest? It's up to you to determine that your own daughters, if you have any, will not be bound to them as you were, and as your mother and grandmother were before you.

If you think I have a point-by-point blueprint for you, or easy answers for the many concerns and problems you as a grown daughter face with your mother, I'm afraid you will be disappointed. What this book will do is offer some guidelines that may help you take a new and closer look at what is going on between you and your mom. Perhaps it also will help you to see your situation in a new, more understanding light. My hope is that in the process of understanding yourself better and understanding your mother better, you will come to a closer adult friendship with her.

Your relationship to your mother is influenced by many factors. By looking at these various factors, perhaps you can gain some awareness of how they have shaped your particular relationship. Part I will help you examine how birth order, patterns of relating, and differing personalities affect your relationship to your mother.

But becoming aware of the dynamics of your relationship is only one step. Your awareness probably will lead you to change in several areas. Part II will help you work through changes such as gaining independence from your mother, handling conflict with her, making peace, and becoming friends. It also will help you explore friendship with your mother in unusual or difficult situations. If your mother is not a Christian, or if you were raised in a dysfunctional home that included an alcoholic mother or physical or emotional abuse, you will need to consider some unique dynamics of your relationship with your mother. Or if you are trying to make friends with a stepmother—in addition to or instead of your birth mother—you may need some help sorting through ways you can bring unity and harmony to your relationship. Finally, Part II will help you anticipate some of the unique problems and opportunities in dealing with your aging mother.

I hope that the principles and suggestions in this book will help you find answers to some of the questions that may be bothering you. I also hope that you will gain a new loving respect for your mother and a better understanding of why she is the way she is. Most of all, I hope and pray that both you and your mother will learn to reach out to each other and move beyond an outgrown mommy-child relationship into a much more appropriate and enjoyable relationship as loving, adult friends.

To this end, I wish you happy reading.

PART I.
GAINING AWARENESS

1.

How Is Your Relationship with Your Mother?

Though I find it hard to believe—and even harder to admit—I'm a middle-aged woman. Except when I'm with my mother, that is. Then I'm a ten-year-old tomboy. Or sometimes I'm an awkward and clumsy thirteen-year-old. Or I'm sixteen and struggling to find myself. Once in a while I'm a naughty four-year-old getting my hand slapped. Isn't it strange how such transformations happen to grown daughters?

Last fall, on our way back to Michigan where my daughter, Lisa, is a college student, Lisa and I spent a night at my parents' house. My mother and daughter and I were sitting around the kitchen table—Lisa on one side of me, my mother on the other—when Mom started telling me about a new hairstyle she thought would look perfect on me. Nervously I patted down an unruly lock of hair and stammered out an explanation of how it usually looked better than this but . . . I had slipped into my thirteen-year-old, insecure self. What a shock suddenly to realize that I was the youngest person at the table!

Mothers and daughters. What a strange and incomprehensible relationship we have.

WHAT IS YOUR RELATIONSHIP
WITH YOUR MOTHER?

What happens when you think about your mother? What are your most endearing memories of the two of you together? What are the recollections that pierce you most deeply? How do you react when someone says, "You remind me of your mom"?

"My mother is a very special person," Susan told me. "I have such happy memories of my childhood, especially of my teen years. I never knew adolescence was supposed to be different or difficult. I sailed through and enjoyed sharing my thoughts and activities with my mom. We had a trust that seemed so normal, I never thought to question it."

"Not all of us were fortunate enough to have a loving, caring, supportive mother," said Barbara. "When I was growing up, I felt totally alone. I was sure no one had ever experienced what I was going through."

"My mother loved me," Leslie said. "I never seriously doubted that. The problem was that we had nothing in common. It was as if we were from different universes. We lived in the same house, but we operated in totally separate worlds."

"I was the tail-end baby of my family," said Tamara. "By the time I was born, my mother was burned out on mothering. I just sort of grew up. If I was ever mothered by anyone, it was by my older sisters."

If you're like most daughters, you tend to swing between sentimental memories and angry recollections, between remembrances of tenderness and disappointment, between memories of love and pain. You may have bitter memories, perhaps even of neglect or abuse.

YOUR EXPECTATIONS OF YOUR MOTHER

Motherhood is surrounded by certain expectations that place great demands on moms. Mothers are expected to be selfless, all-loving, all-providing, endlessly comforting, infinitely wise and understanding, eternally reassuring, and always supportive. Who can be such a person? Yet as a result of these false expectations, these images of the "perfect mother," many daughters grow up thinking, *Boy, was I cheated!*

It's unfair to compare your mother or your childhood with some romantic ideal. The fact is, no mother is perfect, and no childhood is perfect.

Take some time to reflect on your early years. As you consider each event, ask yourself, "How did I feel about that?" Be as honest and objective as you can. This will help you make some profitable judgments about your childhood.

When your expectations of what a "good mother" should be do not meet the reality of what you see in your mom, you may find yourself being critical and resentful of her. You may be tempted to blame her for her actions.

We Americans believe strongly in the relationship between cause and effect. For anything that happens, we think, there has to be a cause. In recent years it has become popular to blame parents—especially mothers—for whatever problems their children have in life. When we see a problem within ourselves, it's easy to say, "It's not my fault! It's because of the way I was raised."

But laying blame is an unproductive exercise. How much more profitable it is to recognize the things that need to be changed within ourselves, then to set about changing them. And that we can do.

You have a choice to make: Will you follow the examples set by your mother, or will you reject those examples and set your own course? Will you work toward accepting and building on the positive in her and learning from and improving on the not-so-positive?

So your mother is not all she could be. So she made mistakes when you were growing up. *You can't change the past.* But you can change the present, and you can pave the way for a better future.

THE BASIC EXPECTATION

One of the most basic expectations we have of our mothers is that they love us—always, no matter what, for all time.

In the apostle Paul's letter to Titus, he instructs mothers to love their children (2:4). It seems to be a strange command, doesn't it? Isn't love a natural thing for a mother to give her child? We are raised to believe that mother love is different from other kinds of love. Mother love isn't open to mistakes or doubts or ambivalence. It's always there, no matter what. Mothers just naturally love their children. It comes with the territory.

Unfortunately, that idea is an illusion. Like any other affection—except *agape* love, which comes from God himself—mother love is imperfect. The reality is that not all mothers *do* love their children—at least not in a way the child can recognize. If you had that kind of mother, perhaps you, like many other women, grew up convinced that your mother didn't love you at all.

It's devastating to grow up feeling unloved. It's terrible to be an adult daughter and still feel you must struggle to get your mother to love you. This is the ultimate in rejection.

On the other hand, it may not have been a lack of love at all. It may be simply a matter of perception. One of the problems is that we daughters want our mothers to love us in ways that are meaningful to us. When they express their love in ways different from how we feel we need to be loved, we can come to the false conclusion that our mothers don't love us.

Carla grew up believing she was unloved. And because she felt unloved, she was convinced she must be unlovable. Worst of all, she was sure it was all her fault. She never discussed her feelings with her mother, and she never made any attempt to understand her mother or the reason for her mom's actions.

"Why should I?" Carla asked. "I know she doesn't care. What more is there to know?"

There's a lot more to know. It's important that we learn to see our mothers as whole persons, mixtures of both good and bad, success and failure, wisdom and error. Only then can we hope to see the resulting relationship as one brought about by two caring people working together.

Facing Illusions

When we were young children, we believed our parents were perfect. If anything was wrong, it had to have been our fault because it certainly couldn't have been theirs. Kids have to believe that. They are too totally dependent on their parents to allow themselves to doubt their parents' actions. As children, we can't afford to be angry with our mothers, so we turn our anger against ourselves. Instead of saying, "She is bad," we say, "I am bad." In our childish eyes, mother *has* to be all-wise and ever-kind.

Maybe you are like Carla. Maybe you not only feel unloved but also feel that your unloveliness is your fault. May I share a freeing truth with you? Whatever your mother felt about you, it was *not* your fault. No child should ever have to earn her mother's love. When you were born—or perhaps adopted—into your family, you received the right to be loved simply because you were a part of that family. It should have made no difference whether you were cute or funny looking, a girl or a boy, tiny or large, feminine or tomboyish, musical or athletic, or none of these. You deserved to be loved just because you were you.

The most extreme example of a child's need to believe in her all-loving mother is found with battered children. When I was a teenager, my parents cared for foster children. For her entire life, nine-year-old Eileen had been abused, neglected, and physically mistreated by her alcoholic mother. Things got so bad that Eileen finally was taken out of her home and brought to us.

Eileen's mother was always making extravagant promises to her, but without fail, she would let the little girl down. Eileen's mother lied to her, stole from her, and broke every promise she ever made. Yet when Eileen talked about her mother, it was always in glowing, loving terms. However cruel, however hurtful, however unloving her mother might have been, Eileen never attempted to hide the fact that she longed to go back and live with her.

Stronger than the desire to be free of pain and abuse, stronger than the instinct for life itself, is a child's need to perpetuate the illusion that she has a good mother who truly cares about her. And as the child grows up, the adult she becomes continues to be driven to believe the illusion.

For other children, the illusion is different. Mark Twain once observed, "When I was a boy of fourteen, my father was so ignorant I could hardly stand to have the old man around. But when I got to be twenty-one, I was astonished at how much that old man had learned in seven years."

What Is Love, Anyway?

Most mothers do love their children. But even loving mothers sometimes do not *like* their kids. The same mother who wouldn't hesitate to put her body between her child and a runaway freight train often finds herself resenting the day-by-day demands her child places on her time, finances, and lifestyle. And though she probably never realizes it, her child senses her frustration and resentments.

The good news is that there *is* real love between most mothers and daughters. But there is bad news too: It may not be the kind of love we want it to be. It may not be the kind of love everyone expects us to feel. And it may not be the kind of love we pretend it to be.

The problem starts with the word *love*. It's so ambiguous. Everyone seems to interpret it differently. Is it any wonder that it's such an overworked word?

"I love you. I'm doing this for your own good," a

mother says when she forbids her daughter to play with a friend. Or, "If I didn't love you so much, I wouldn't make you wear this coat." Or, "Of course I love you. That's why I'm making you go to camp. I want you with me, but it's better for you to enjoy a summer of fresh air and exercise and fun activities."

Each of these explanations seems reasonable on the surface. And we desperately want to believe that everything our mothers do is motivated by love. But the fact is, what is expressed in these phrases is often not love at all. It may be possessiveness or anxiety. Sometimes it is outright rejection. And even though the child dares not believe this on a conscious level, way down deep she can feel it.

The apostle Paul says some instructive things about love in 1 Corinthians 13. He tells us love is patient and kind, that it neither envies nor boasts. Love is not proud. It is not rude or self-seeking. It is not easily angered nor does it keep a record of wrongs. Love does not delight in evil. Instead, it rejoices in the truth. It always protects, always trusts, always hopes, and always perseveres. And love never fails.

What mother could ever hope to score 100 percent on a list as superb as this? Not one. Not even yours!

Perhaps your mother was good about admiring and praising you and making you feel valued. But what she called love may have been her own need for someone to mother her. If so, you may not have problems with your self-esteem, but you may feel you can't get the closeness and intimacy you need from others. You may believe that other people always let you down.

So many forces, both external and internal, make it difficult for you to be honest and objective about your feelings about your mom. And it often boils down to the familiar accusation: "How can you complain? Just look at all your mother has done for you!"

By the time you are ready to take a hard, honest look at your relationship with your mother, she may have moved on past motherhood to other interests. Or maybe she *hasn't* moved on at all. You may look impatiently at her and see nothing but stagnation. Or perhaps you are considering the relationship only after it has been jerked into your consciousness by the sight of your mom suffering from the frailties of advancing age or diminishing health. If so, your feelings may be colored by guilt.

No matter how you were raised or what your mother did wrong, it is never too late for you to change any of your life patterns or attitudes. You can grow and learn. You can adapt, and you can change.

Do you want things to be different between you and your mother? Do you long for a closer relationship between the two of you? Do you want to move from being a little girl and her mommy to being two adult friends? Then you will need to make some changes.

The place to start is with yourself. As you come to understand yourself better, you will be able to assess where you may need to change.

2.

Birth Order

Carolyn, Ruthanne, and Nancy are sisters. But to listen to them talk about their childhood experiences, you would never guess they were raised by the same mother.

"Nancy was always playing the sweet little thing," said Carolyn. "She got all kinds of love and attention from Mom. It was different for me. I don't remember ever getting so much as a good-night kiss from my mother."

Nancy disagrees vehemently. "It was Carolyn who always got special privileges. Mother explained that it was because Carolyn was the oldest. To Mom, I was always too little to do anything or go anywhere."

"All I know," says Ruthanne, "is that everyone was favored but me. I wasn't the oldest, I wasn't the youngest, I wasn't the smartest, I wasn't the cutest, I wasn't the anythingist. I was just plain old boring me."

BETTER, WORSE, OR JUST DIFFERENT?

"Being the first child is definitely the worst," insisted Ellen, the oldest of six. "I never really got a childhood. With five younger brothers and sisters, Mother always put me in charge of this or that. I was stuck with a lot of responsibility. I got so tired of being 'mommy's little helper' and 'setting a good example for the little ones'! Let me tell you, the pressure of being the oldest is terrible. I know. I've been there."

Ellen's younger sister sees it differently. "Ellen was the only child in our family who got real time and attention from Mom. After Ellen, my mother was too busy to spend much time with any of the rest of us. If my sister thinks she had it bad, she should try being the second child. I spent my whole childhood trying to catch up to her!"

Does the oldest daughter get an extra dose of intelligence and ambitious perseverance from a mother determined to do everything right? Or does she just get burdened down with too much pressure and responsibility at too early an age? Is the middle child doomed to forever play the catch-up game? Or does she emerge into adulthood a more creative, free person? Is the baby of the family more often carefree and full of fun, or is she likely to develop into an irresponsible, maybe even manipulative adult?

These are good questions. And though they have been endlessly studied and researched over the years, even the psychologists and researchers are still debating the answers.

Obviously, birth order is only one of many important variables, all of which work together to shape an individual's personality. And yet it is one variable that doesn't change. No matter what else you become in life, you will always be your mother's first child, a middle daughter, or her baby. If you grew up your mother's only child, her only child is what you will always be.

WHAT ARE THE VARIABLES?

The effects your birth order had on you and your relationship to your mother are influenced by many variables. One variable is the spacing between you and any siblings. If you are a middle child who is only a few years older than the baby, for instance, your traits may be more those of a youngest child than of a middle child.

A second variable is the sex of the children in your family. Girls, for instance, are much more likely to be expected to take charge of the household and to care for younger brothers and sisters. If you had an older brother, your traits may be closer to those of an oldest child, even though you are not the oldest.

A third variable is the expectation level your mother placed on you and your brothers and sisters. "I have two older brothers," says Leslie. "Being the only girl, the one my mother longed for and patiently prayed for, was a much stronger determinant of how she raised me than the fact that I was her youngest child."

"It's not that birth order *causes* certain kinds of personalities to develop," says Robert L. Powers, chairman of the Americas Institute of Adlerian Studies in Chicago. "It's just that in certain situations, some things are more likely to happen than others."

Many experts agree that every little girl enters life looking for her own special place into which she, and only she, can fit. When you were a tiny child, you wanted—and needed—an identity all your own. Once you squirmed into that niche, you began a search for a way to get the biggest share of your mother's love and attention. It may be that it was your order of birth that influenced the vantage point from which you viewed these challenges and how you decided to handle them.

The following compilation of general birth-order categories and the dynamics involved in each might help you understand not only why you are the way you are but also why you and your mother react to each other the way you do. The categories are the firstborn child, the middle child, the youngest child, and the only child.

But first a disclaimer: remember, these are only general guidelines. Some of them may fit you, but others won't. Don't look at this as a science, just a rough measuring stick. So stand up straight and tall and see how the guidelines fit.

WHERE DO YOU FIT?

Firstborn Daughter

If you were a firstborn child, you were a lucky girl indeed. For a while you had your mommy all to yourself. Whether you rolled over or said your first word or took your first toddling steps, Mommy was surely convinced you were the cleverest, sweetest, most precocious child in the whole world—and the cutest to boot!

What was the result of all this doting attention? You probably grew up feeling you really *were* important, that people always would be interested in your ideas and thoughts—in short, that people would always be interested in *you.*

However, the firstborn child faces disadvantages too. As Ellen points out, mothers often expect a lot from their oldest daughters. This puts great pressure on oldest daughters. How can they ever manage to live up to their mothers' high expectations and standards?

To make things worse, for many firstborn daughters, just when they thought they had life under control, something monumental happened: A new baby arrived. Suddenly the firstborn daughter was no longer her mama's star. If you are like many firstborn daughters, you may have reacted by whipping yourself into action, determined to regain your place in your mother's eyes. You may have tried to imitate the baby, but you quickly found out that didn't work. Mothers take a dim view of three-year-olds who want bottles or five-year-olds who revert to thumb sucking and baby talk. "You're not a baby!" Mama probably scolded. "You're a big girl now."

Many firstborn daughters find it effective to align themselves with their mothers. "It's up to you to set a good example for the baby," Mama tells her. "I need you to help me take care of her." Sound familiar?

Sure, this all may have helped to make a leader of you,

but it also may have put a great deal of pressure on you to grow up too early. It's not uncommon for firstborn daughters to be so intent on being good "big girls," helping Mommy, and doing things right that they never learn to have fun being children.

If you were the firstborn child, you may have found the territorial waters rough. But remember, your mother was dealing with parenthood for the first time. She hadn't yet learned to pull back and take a wide view of things. How could she not make mistakes? But you also were her first child-love. You will always have a special place in her heart—a place no one will ever share with you. You were her firstborn!

Middle Daughter

Poor middle children! We hear and read much about their unenviable plight. And, indeed, if you were a middle child, you surely did have the most uncertain position in the family. Mothers tend to get caught up with their oldest and their youngest, so middle kids really can end up feeling left out and unimportant.

"My mother loved Jeannette because Jeannette was her oldest," said Kathryn, a second daughter. "She loved Leanne because Leanne was her baby. And she loved David because he was her only boy. She didn't have any reason to love me."

Because your position as a middle child was less clearly defined, you may have looked outside your family for an identity of your own. "When anything happens, my sisters and brother want to go home," Kathryn continued. "Not me. I love my mom and all, but she's not where I get my support. I go to my friends."

Do middle daughters love their mothers any less? No. But because they tend to depend less on their moms, the painful process of breaking loose may be easier for middle kids.

Another characteristic of middle children is that they are often good empathizers. They know what it feels like to be younger ("You can't go with your sister. You're too little") and what it feels like to be older ("It's your fault. You're older, so it's up to you to set an example"). Middle daughters may become very good at negotiating and making peace—a wonderful asset when it comes to making friends with their mothers. Or middle daughters may become very competitive, figuring that only by pushing and fighting can they ever hope to get their rightful share of anything— which can make friendship with their mothers more difficult.

An added challenge for you as a follow-up child—even if you were the youngest—was to find a special identity for yourself. In most families, two children do not play the same role. If the first child has already claimed the part of the athlete or the straight-A student or the artist, the second child will seek some other way to be unique. This drive to be special often comes out in small, unexpected ways— sometimes to the exasperation of the mother. If your older sibling was neat, for instance, you may have asserted your individuality by being a real slob.

If your mother set particularly rigid expectations for her children, you may have had some serious conflict with your older sibling. If you felt excellent grades were the only thing that mattered to your mother, for instance, and your older brother was already getting them, you may have found yourself faced with a real dilemma: What was Mom going to find special about you? If you couldn't find a place for yourself through acceptable channels, you may have turned to making trouble. Child-development specialists tell us that second children are often more rebellious, more questioning, more willing to bend—or break—the rules than are their older siblings.

When your mother looks at you today, she probably sees some version of what she saw in your childhood days. Were you a non-conformist or a rebel? Were you the eternal peacemaker? Were you a fighter? Whatever you were back then may be what she still sees in you today.

The Baby

Only the baby in the family doesn't have to worry about a brother or sister coming up from behind and threatening her position. No wonder the youngest has the reputation of growing up to be carefree and easygoing.

If you were the last-born child, you probably were more indulged by your mother and less bound by her rules than were your older siblings. Perhaps you even grew up to be a bit of a show-off. Early on, you learned you weren't likely to get your way by pushing or insisting. How could you? Everyone else was bigger and stronger. So you may have learned to depend on your charm to get your way. Many youngest children become skillful manipulators, a trait they carry on into their adult years. Could it be that even today you are trying to manipulate your mother? Manipulation is not a good foundation on which to build a strong friendship.

One of the biggest problems for many youngest children lies in the area of responsibility. The very same mother who always told her firstborn daughter she was "a big girl" encourages her youngest to be cute and dependent. It's so hard for mothers to see their littlest grow up. When the "baby" *does* grow up, she may continue to expect her mother to take care of her and solve her problems. The "baby" may insist she wants to be independent, but her actions may reveal that she still clings tightly to her mother. Is this you? If so, it's time to loosen your grip. It's time to learn to take care of yourself.

The Only Child

An only child is a firstborn child who never lost her privileged place in her family. An only daughter has some real advantages. She often grows up secure and self-assured. Why shouldn't she? She never had to compete for her mother's love and attention.

Only children, even when they are very young, often are comfortable with adults. If you are an only child, you may feel more comfortable with your mother, more able to communicate with and understand her, than some of your friends are with their mothers.

UNDERSTANDING YOURSELF

Again, birth-order profiles such as these are generalizations, and as such they are fraught with exceptions. So why should you consider the subject at all? For one very important reason: it will help you understand your beginnings. And understanding where you started can help you to understand where you are today. It may also help you to make sense of where you are with your mother and where you can go from here.

3.

Same Old Troupe, Same Old Performance

I'll never forget Mrs. Smithson, Carolee's mother. Now there was a perfect mom. She wore seersucker pedal pushers and saddle oxfords. (My mom wore housedresses and sensible shoes.) Carolee's mother filled us up with Hershey bars and Oreo cookies. (If we got any snacks from my mom, they were homemade and healthy.) Carolee's mom gave us firm yellow bananas with just a touch of green. (My mom's bananas were soft and black-speckled.) For carrying out the trash, Carolee received praise and a generous allowance. (I helped with the cleaning and cooking and washed endless stacks of dishes. My pay? "The satisfaction of knowing you've helped the family"—my mother's words.)

Few of my friends' moms came close to having Mrs. Smithson's class and perfection. Yet even the least of my friends' mothers had one enviable quality—they all had the decency to stay out of sight. Everyone's mother was either flawless or invisible. Everyone's, that is, except mine. At least that's how it seemed to me when I was an insecure adolescent. It was downright embarrassing.

What was your relationship with your mom like when you were an adolescent? What were your patterns of behavior? How did you both deal with your growing need for independence, for example?

Independence is a strange thing. Mothers want the best

for their daughters. They want their children to have better lives than they had, to be happier, more successful, more fulfilled. But mothers also have a fear: "What if, as my daughter grows and develops and becomes successful, she leaves me behind?"

Most mothers feel a strong desire to see their children grow into strong, independent, responsible people. But many mothers also subconsciously wish that their children remain weak and dependent. The way in which your mother balanced these opposing desires was important to your development. If her wishes for your independence were stronger, you are undoubtedly reaping the benefits today. If her wishes for you to be dependent and inadequate were the dominant ones, you are probably paying for it now.

DOUBLE MESSAGES

Thinking back to your adolescence, you may remember times when your mother seemed to be making contradictory demands on you. If your mother said to you, "Your grades are good, dear, but you could do better," she may have been making a simple statement of fact. But she also may have been handing out a double message that is both approving and undermining.

Presented with her double message, you probably felt locked into a double bind. If you obeyed one demand, you would be disobeying the other. For instance, your mom may have said, "Do it your way, but don't come crying to me when everything falls apart." What she really was saying was, "I want you to be self-reliant, so do as I say." Either way, you lost. A pretty miserable situation, wasn't it?

Double messages create conflict because they use guilt as a way of saying, "Don't grow up and leave me." Many double messages belittle and intimidate, leaving the child with feelings of inadequacy that keep her hobbled for life.

Anna knows all about being hobbled. She says it's as if her mother is right there with her all the time. Although

mother has had on you—whether it's her love for music, her easygoing nature, her ability to make guests feel at ease, her contagious sense of humor, her ability to face a crisis with courage, her unyielding faith in God, or her love for the outdoors—affirm her for those contributions. Tell her how much you appreciate what she has passed on to you. Write her a letter or write a note on her Mother's Day card and express what positive influence she has had on you. Not only will she appreciate knowing how you feel, but also you will become closer to her by articulating those feelings.

When you recognize how much you are like your mother, you have a choice. You can chafe about the negative influence and blame her for it, or you can choose to change. Remember, you can't go back and change your past, and you can't change who your mother is now. But you can choose what you will do with her influence on you. You can try to balance the negative influences with the positive ones, and you can try to change in yourself the negative habits and behavior you have picked up from her.

Making those changes won't be easy, but change *is* possible. The next few chapters will explore various ways of bringing about possible changes in your relationship with your mother.

PART II.
MAKING CHANGES

5.

Breaking Free

In order to make friends with your mother, you may need to break free from some old patterns of relating. You'll need to become an independent person. Unfortunately, that's easier said than done.

Now you understand more about who you are and where you came from. And you have some idea of the things you want to see changed in yourself. You are ready to stretch out of that confining mold your mother has set for you.

You have already decided what you *don't* want to do. But do you know exactly what you want to replace those traits with? In other words, do you understand what it is in that particular behavior or action that makes it objectionable to you?

Almost anyone you ask will insist she wants to be her own person. You probably would say the same. But are you really serious about once-and-for-all becoming independent? If so, here are some specific steps you should consider.

MAKE SURE YOU WANT TO BE INDEPENDENT

Sure, independence sounds great, but you should be aware that it comes with a price. Being independent will surely mean making some difficult changes in your life. If you want your mother to treat you as an adult, you will have to give up your childhood luxuries—like the free house-cleaning and laundry services your mom always provided and all those great home-cooked meals.

Emotional dependence can also be very appealing. Do you tend to run home to Mama for help whenever you have a problem? To be truly independent, you will need to take on the responsibility of dealing with your problems yourself. You also will have to be willing to give up the benefit of financial dependence. No more taking advantage of your mother's open purse whenever you run short of money.

The thing to remember is this: As long as you cling to your childish role, you have no right to expect your mother to relinquish her mothering role. If you keep yourself dependent, you have no right to clamor for independence.

CARVE OUT YOUR OWN IDENTITY

The end result is that your struggle to achieve genuine independence is sure to be riddled with confusion and uncertainty. You need to carve out your own identity, yet you desperately want to hang on to your mother's approval. Moving into a true adult role is difficult. It's tough to separate yourself from the feeling that you are merely a copy of your mother and to move on to where you are able to find out who you really are.

Of course you want to please your mother. And you want to make your time with her enjoyable for both of you. There's certainly nothing wrong with that. The problem, you see, is one of boundaries. Remember, to be separate from your mother, you must carve out your own separate identity. Things must not continue on the way they have been throughout the years. If your Mom comments that your gifts are too expensive or too cheap or the wrong color, say cheerfully, "I saved the receipts so you could exchange them." If she complains that your kids have no table manners, smile and say, "I learned from you to continue setting a good example. They'll learn." When she says your face isn't right for long hair and you'd look better with a short cut, say, "You may be right, but I surely do like the versatility of long hair. I think I'll keep it this way a while longer." Then change the subject. Guess what! You are now the one in control!

DETERMINE FOR YOURSELF WHO YOU ARE

Some of us grow up obsessed with being good daughters. We devote ourselves to living up to our mothers' ideas of how we should look, what our interests should be, how we ought to behave. "As long as I can remember," Lynda says, "my goal was to talk, dress, behave, even think like my mother wanted me to."

Others of us focused on what pleased our mothers, then purposely did the opposite. "That was me," Rosemary agrees. "Even today, if Mom tells me about something that is 'perfect' for me, I immediately hate it."

Do you see yourself in either Lynda or Rosemary? If you are at one extreme or the other, you are giving your mother too much authority over you. You need to take your focus off her. By trying so desperately to be "good" or "bad," you are in effect refusing to set your own standards. The result is sure to be anger at your mother and guilt at yourself. If you are ever to stop blaming your mother for everything that displeases or disappoints you about yourself, you must decide who you are and then accept the responsibility for yourself.

No matter what you do, no matter how perfectly you do it, you may find that you and your mother still will not see eye-to-eye on many matters. That's okay. You probably always will have differences between you. But there's nothing wrong with differences.

If those differences cause conflict between you, you need to work on those conflicts. If you do, things are bound to improve. And believe it or not, the time may come when in all honesty you can look your mother in the eye and say, "You know what, Mom? I really like you!"

Find Other Role Models

One thing that may help you break out of the pattern set for you by your mother is to find additional role models. Do you know women who have traits you especially admire? Ones whose love and caring are apparent? Ones who impress you with their gentleness or perseverance or dependability or acceptance? Listen to those women as they speak. Watch how they act.

But don't expect your role models to be perfect. They, like the rest of us, have faults. The point is to find the positive within each of them and then to practice it yourself.

Communicate Who You Are

Once you understand who you are as a person, communicate that to your mother. Let her know what is important to you. It's only fair to be honest and open with her. If you haven't talked to her about your need for a different type of relationship, how can you blame her for not understanding?

Speaking up may be a difficult thing to do. It may involve more than merely explaining your feelings and emphasizing to your mother how much you need to put a bit of distance between the two of you. You may have to establish some guidelines—both for yourself and for her. You even may have to set some limits.

Usually the direct approach is best. Say what you have to say, but do it with love and without anger. It will be easier if you choose a time when you are not rushed or tired or pressured or already upset. Your mother needs to know for sure that you love her and that you still need her love.

It may be easier to encourage your mother to loosen her grip on you if you assure her that your move toward independence does not mean that everything will come to an end between you. Help her to see that a change actually can be the beginning of a healthier, more pleasant relationship.

CHANGE ROLES

So now the big question: Once you have been cast in the family drama, how can you change your role?

The bad news is that change doesn't come easily or quickly. We live in a society that expects instant cures, dinner in minutes, and solutions within an hour (not counting commercials). You probably will find that changing your role, changing something that deeply ingrained, can be a difficult process. And it can be painful for everyone involved.

The good news is that change is possible. It can be done.

If you are serious about turning in your negative script—and in so doing, possibly rewriting the entire drama for the whole family along more positive lines—here are some suggestions:

Become Aware

Barbara tells about her family's usual Sunday-morning routine. They would always get up late. Everyone would be rushing around and competing for the shower. As the morning progressed, tempers flared. By the time the family got into the car, Dad was sulking and Mom was angry and scolding.

All the way to church, Barbara's parents would yell at each other and scream at the kids. But as her dad pulled into the church parking lot, there was an instantaneous change. Barbara's parents would climb out of the car, smiling, waving, and greeting their friends. Mom would take Barbara's hand and put her arm around Dad.

"I hated the hypocrisy!" Barbara says. "I vowed it would never be that way in my family."

It isn't. Barbara dropped out of church when she was in high school and has never been back.

Barbara knew a change was in order. And she did accomplish her goal of avoiding the trait she so disliked in her mother. But her choice of alternate behavior is no better.

Breaking out of the old role should be only part of your goal. It is just as important to choose a positive replacement.

It is only when you become aware of the drama you and your mom are playing out so convincingly that you can begin to change the script. The thing that makes it so tough is that the entire production is performed unconsciously.

Perhaps you have gained some insight from the list of possible mother roles and positive daughter roles examined in chapter 3. Now try listing the complaints you have about your relationship to your mother. What does she do that drives you crazy? How do you respond to her actions? When you anticipate being together, do you dread some specific thing? Even though both you and she may be playing more than one role, try to isolate the one that is causing you the most trouble. You can always come back later and work on the others.

Now spend some time with your mother. Try to observe yourself as you both step into your respective roles. Don't try to change anything yet, just watch. (Note: It also may help to observe the way you operate with your friends, your husband, your children, or your co-workers. You just may be playing out the same role with them.)

Are you beginning to recognize any specific patterns? Great! That means you're on the right track. But insight is just a starting point. From there you need to move on to the next step.

Rewrite the Script

Gaining insight was the easy part. Now you're ready for the hard part. Begin this step by recognizing that nobody likes change. Leaving what is familiar is always scary. And it involves risk. No matter how painful and restrictive your family role might be, it's going to be hard to trade in the security of its familiarity for a role that is unknown and untested. No, it won't be easy. But it will be worth the effort!

Decide what you want to change. Be specific here. Write out your complaints in detail. Then look at your list and see if you can find a way to turn each item into a positive suggestion for yourself. For instance, you may have written: "I hate the way my mother criticizes my clothes." Next to that you might write: "When I'm with her, I'll make a point of wearing an outfit I think she will like. If she still criticizes, I'll simply say, 'Really? I've always liked this dress.' Then I'll change the subject."

Refuse to respond as if you were a child. You will become a victim of your mother's criticism only if you allow yourself to be victimized. If you hate to go home because every time you do, your mom treats you like a ten-year-old, the real problem may not be your mother so much as the fact that you respond to her as if you were ten. Don't wait until your mother stops treating you like a ten-year-old. Start the process yourself by refusing to respond to her as if you were a child. The best thing you can do for yourself—and for your mother as well—is to do all you can to establish an adult-to-adult relationship to her.

Some mothers will try forever to keep their daughters childlike. If this is true of your mom, your challenge will be to learn to respond to her in a mature, independent way, even in the midst of her resistance.

Understand that you are no longer a child. Recognize

the truth that you don't have to keep on playing that role. Are you in the habit of always asking Mom for her opinion? Perhaps it's time to stop. The less you depend on her approval, the more you will be able to avoid arguments and hard feelings.

On those occasions when the two of you do have disagreements, remember that it's your responsibility to set your boundaries. Then insist that you both stay within them. You might say, "I know you don't want me to change jobs. We've been through all that several times. But this is a decision I have to make for myself. If you have something new to add to the discussion, fine. Otherwise, I don't want to talk about it anymore."

Move slowly. You can change yourself, but you can't do it overnight. Don't expect to. You have spent a lifetime walking through your part and memorizing your lines. You have rehearsed them over and over with your mother. It's going to take a long time to get used to being recast into a different role. And it's going to take time for your mother to recognize you in your new role and to figure out how she is to react to it.

Set realistic goals. No matter how determined you are, from time to time you are going to slip back into the old routine. Expect it. And when it happens, don't let it throw you. Concentrate instead on the progress you're making. And don't be surprised if your old negative feelings hang on for a while. As you persist toward your goal, those feelings will weaken. In time they may disappear completely.

Now do it! People quickly tire of listening to other people talk about what they are going to do. Even worse, too much talking can take the place of actually getting busy and doing something. Only action brings results. Share your plans if you want to, but let your actions speak more loudly than your words.

Be willing to take control of your relationship. I realize that control can be a volatile word. But the thing is, you are the one who should set the direction and tone of your relationship along a smooth, healthy course. It doesn't mean you have to be bossy or demanding or bullying toward your mother. And it certainly doesn't mean you need to be defiant. Tantrums and major scenes are not adult behavior, and they won't gain your mom's cooperation. Remember, your goal is to have her see and respect and respond to you as an adult. It's hard to expect such a result if your behavior is childish.

GAIN FINANCIAL AND EMOTIONAL FREEDOM

In our society, breaking loose is not nearly as automatic and natural a procedure as it is in other cultures. In our culture, grown children gain freedom in two ways: financially and emotionally.

Financial Freedom

Independence involves earning enough money to care for yourself. It means being able to make your own decisions and to accept responsibility for the consequences without always turning to Mom for help. While you certainly can ask for her advice, independence means you don't burden your mother down with your financial problems. And it means you don't blame her for your financial mistakes.

Emotional Freedom

Freedom also involves becoming emotionally free from your mom. And that's not always easy to do. It was time to leave for our drive up north for my parents' fiftieth wedding anniversary celebration, and I still wasn't packed. It's not that I hadn't started in time. I had been packing and changing my mind and unpacking and repacking for two days.

Frantically, I started hunting through my closet yet again. My new green dress was nice, but would Mom think it was too tight? I had a pink dress I never liked, but she had seen it and remarked how pretty it was. Should I wear that pink dress even though I would feel uncomfortable and out of place? My yellow dress was certainly out. Too austere for Mom's taste. My blue sun dress was a possibility—she'd like the fact that I had made it myself. But, I wasn't sure. My flowered skirt and red blouse, maybe? Mom liked ruffles.

Suddenly it hit me. It wasn't the anniversary party that was the problem. *I* was the problem.

Whenever I buy anything—in fact, whenever I wear anything or do anything—something goes off inside my head, telling me what my mother would think of it. For over forty years I've been buying, baking, mothering, cooking, sewing, doing, and striving to win my mother's approval.

Pretty silly, isn't it? A middle-aged woman who still conducts her life to please a woman who lives five hundred miles away? But I suspect I'm not all that unusual. A lot of us still lug around an awful lot of leftover parental baggage. Probably you have some of your own baggage.

Being emotionally independent means you feel free to be yourself. Ideally, you will thoughtfully and prayerfully choose a direction based on your own particular abilities and inclinations and on the opportunities open to you. As you carefully consider your parents' ideas and advice about your vocation, your lifestyle, the values and beliefs you accept, the way you spend your money, and the friendships you form, you understand that in the end, all these choices are yours and yours alone.

Gain approval. Once upon a time, before my mother would arrive for a visit, I would scrub my house from top to bottom. I would finish the little dress I was sewing for my daughter, lay in a store of special foods, do as much weeding as I possibly could in the garden, struggle to revive the dying house plants, bathe the dog, and sweep the walkways. Not that it really mattered. Mom didn't seem to notice the sparkling house or my daughter's new dress or the swept walks, and she would be on a diet that didn't include the special foods I had planned. Instead, she would suggest I trim the houseplants and re-weed the garden. Then she would ask if "that smelly dog" really needed to be in the house. I would in turn be disappointed, frustrated, insulted, and defensive.

If you're like me and most every other daughter in the country, no one can get a rise out of you faster than your mother, even if you are devoted to her, even if you're an ideal daughter and she's a wonderful mother. You love her, but she can drive you crazy. When your mother arrives, it all hits you at once: kisses and control, hugs and guilt.

Despite the considerable distance you seem to have put between yourself and your mother, regardless of the separate and different lives you may now be living, you probably still are trying desperately to please Mom and to make her proud of you. And in many, many ways, your mother is still clinging tightly to you.

It may be that the reason you continue to cling to your mother on her terms is because you so badly need her approval. But you can find approval from other people. Your mother is not the only person who can give you the support and acceptance you crave. A close female friend may be the best choice, or a sister or cousin or perhaps a co-worker. Or you may find that you can count on gaining approval from your husband, if you are married. The important thing is to choose someone whom you really like and who really likes you—someone who approves of you and accepts you just as you are.

If you can find adequate approval from other people, you won't need to rely so heavily on your mother's approval. You will be more free in how you relate to her.

Develop self-confidence. "I'm dreading Christmas," Kathryn said. "I know I won't be able to make my mother happy. She'll criticize the gifts I choose. She won't like the way my kids behave. She'll chide me for not eating my sweet potatoes even though she knows I've always hated them. And she'll tell me my hair needs to be cut."

If your mother continues to undermine your confidence ("You would look so much prettier if you cut your hair"), your intelligence ("That's a pretty silly thing to do. Are you sure you've really thought it out?"), or your diet ("What do you mean just a small piece? I made this double chocolate cake just for you!"), you need to realize your lack of confidence is more a result of your mother's approach to you than of your approach to her. Don't let her critical words convince you that you are not pretty or not intelligent. Say to yourself, "I like my hair the way it is. My friends like it. My family likes it. I won't let my mother's irritation with my hair influence my own confidence in myself or in my ability to find a flattering hairstyle."

Sometimes unmarried daughters have an even harder time breaking loose and gaining emotional freedom. "Mom always expects me to eat a 'decent' meal—at home, with her and Dad, at six o'clock sharp," Shawna says. "I feel like a ten-year-old who has to come right home from school. And Mother always has an endless list of questions about where I'm going, who I'm going with, and when I'll be home."

Marilyn, a divorced woman of thirty-nine, says, "I'm a legal secretary. My bosses entrust me with all kinds of confidential work. Yet when I'm at my mother's house, she always asks me if I brought any homework along or if I've already got it done!"

Whether you're married, single, or divorced, if your mom refuses to treat you as if you were an adult, you should ask yourself, "Could it be that I'm not acting like a adult?"

You can do very little to achieve a healthy relationship with your mother until you first establish the boundaries of your own independence.

6.
Handling Conflict with Your Mother

If you ever are to succeed at making friends with your mother, you will need to learn to handle the specific areas of conflict that may have built up between you. Do you and your mother have differences of opinion? Do you have unresolved misunderstandings from the past? Are there certain "hot topics" that always bring out the worst in both of you?

Having areas of conflict isn't unusual. We all have them. The real question is, How do you handle your conflict? Do you "tough it out," just hoping you can last through another visit with your mom? Do you blow up? Do you need to prove at all costs that you are right? And perhaps the most important question of all: Can you accept the differences between you?

What about your mother? How does she handle conflict and the differences between you? At the first hint of conflict, some moms try to escape. They may run away—literally. ("Oh, dear, look at the time. I've got to get those dishes washed!") Or they may change the subject. ("Speaking of problems, did I tell you about Sally's daughter, Janet? Well, she met this man . . .") If they are forced to listen, some moms will simply refuse to respond.

Other moms explode. They may yell, insult, threaten, accuse. Some go so far as to break things, kick the dog, even hit people.

Some mothers are so determined to win any conflict that they will resort to bribes ("Let's just forget this and go shopping. I'll buy you a new dress") or ultimatums ("Any more talk like that and you won't be welcome in this house"). Some moms will attempt to dump all the blame on their daughters. ("If you weren't so stubborn, we could have had a close relationship all along"). Some may try to barter their love. ("I love you more when you don't insist on bringing up the past.")

Mothers who tend to be smotherers have their own approach to conflict. They quickly jump up to extinguish any possible uneasiness before it has time to flare into a real conflict. Such a mother may admonish you with something like, "Remember, dear, 'Honor your father and mother.'"

Then there's the mother who has never stopped being critical. You know, the one who's constantly saying, "Why don't you get a better job?" or "I didn't see you in church last Sunday. If you wouldn't stay out so late on Saturday night, you could get up on time on Sunday." Or, "Junior's manners are terrible. You need to spend more time with him." Or, "Your hair is getting long and stringy. You really ought to have it cut."

Sound like your mother? What can you do about it?

Start out by giving your mom the benefit of the doubt. Assume her motives toward you are not malicious. She probably genuinely does want to help you. It's what she's been doing all your life, after all, and she probably can't see herself in any other role. Appreciate her for her good intentions.

Is your mother worried about some upheaval in your life? Is she feeling uncomfortable with you—unwelcome, perhaps, or uncertain of what is expected of her? These kinds of situations can cause a mom to revert to her familiar role of Mommy. Take these possibilities into consideration before you react to her too strongly. It just may be that helping your mother feel more comfortable will solve part of the problem.

Of course, it may be that this isn't the problem at all. It may be that your mother is just too used to running your life and you are too used to letting her do it. The two things you need to say over and over to yourself until you start to believe them are these: "I'm not a child; I'm an adult," and "It's not my job to make my mother happy. She's an adult and is responsible for her own happiness."

Remember, the old routine won't end until you recognize the fact that you are participating in it.

UNDERSTANDING THE ISSUES

The first step in handling conflict with your mother is understanding what kinds of issues and situations spark tension. Perhaps they arise from misperceptions or misunderstandings.

Part of Ellen's conflict with her mother is the result of the different perspective each of them has of their family. "It's as if my mother lives in a totally different world," Ellen says. "When she thinks of our family, she says, 'Someone should make a movie about us. We have so much fun, so many happy times.' I can't believe she could say that! Where was she all those years? I can't believe she doesn't remember!"

Ellen's mother lives with a myth about her family.

Family Myths

"We're a happy family." Maybe your mother is like Ellen's. Although other family members may remember bitter fights, grudges, and resentments, some mothers nevertheless insist on clinging tightly to the myth of having been a happy family.

"We always had bad luck." This myth excuses everyone in the family for every mistake, every failure, every disappointment. Who can be held responsible for simply

being a victim of bad luck? "It wasn't our fault," these family members say. "If only things had been different . . ."

"We all love each other." This myth believes that although the family has had strife, hard feelings, and resentments, if only they can insist that, through it all, they really did—and still do—love each other, then everything is all right. "All the time our girls were growing up, they fought like cats and dogs," one mother says lightly. "But I always knew that, deep down, they loved each other." The fact that the sisters aren't speaking to each other—and haven't for years—is never mentioned.

"No matter how bad things get, we hold our heads high." Pride. That's what this myth is all about. "I remember how I hated wearing my cousin's hand-me-downs," Barbara said. "She was so much bigger than I. I looked terrible and felt worse. I remember one Christmas, each of us kids thought up the gift we most wanted, then we told everyone at school we had actually gotten it. That was Mama's idea. She was afraid if people knew how bad off we were, they would give us 'charity.' To this day, no one in the family ever talks about those hard times. It's as if they never happened."

"Things are what they are. Nothing will ever change." Resignation excuses a family from trying to improve itself. If yours is a family that clings to the myth that nothing will ever change no matter what, you may have a tough time getting your mother's cooperation in working toward a better relationship. Her actions and her attitude, if not her words, will likely say, "That's how we are. Just accept it."

Family myths vary. And different members of the family cling to the myth with different degrees of intensity.

But the myth serves to keep those who accept it blinded to what the people and the interactions within the family are really like. When Ellen's mother talks wistfully about all those good family times, she probably really is telling things the way she remembers them. It's not that she's lying or losing her memory. It's just that she has bought into the "We are a happy family" myth, and she is clinging to it for dear life.

Actually, family myths can be a positive part of what holds families intact. But if the family clings to an unrealistic or negative family myth, it will reap only negative consequences. Is there evidence that a negative family myth has developed in your family? If you can recognize it for what it is, you have taken a major step toward weakening its hold over you.

Misunderstandings from the Past

Many adult daughters and their mothers have leftover misunderstandings that effectively block or impede the building of a good relationship between them. Here are some of the most common misunderstandings:

Fairness. Every child seems to have a secret yearning to believe that she is her mother's favorite little one. She wants an extra portion of mother's time, attention, and love. But other family members compete for the mother's limited time and attention as well. Many women look at their siblings and harbor convictions like, "Mother wasn't fair. She always loved my sister (or brother) best." And with that conviction goes a good deal of resentment.

Arbitrary discipline. "She'd slap me for nothing," Kathryn says. "It was so unfair. Half the time I never even knew what I'd done wrong." Some mothers are inconsistent or explosive—sometimes even abusive—in their discipline. But more often this complaint arises from a family in which rules were imposed by a mother who failed to listen to her child's side of the story. Kids are very sensitive to unfair treatment—or what they see as unfair treatment. Could it be that a battle based on your mother's discipline still haunts your relationship to her today?

Family secrets. If you knew or suspected that disturbing things were going on in your family—things that no one ever discussed with you honestly—those "family secrets" may be the basis of your present-day battles with your mother. Family secrets often involve financial stress, sexual activity, death, or the fear of a family breakup. Anything that caused your mother distress probably disturbed you too.

Abuse. In some families the "secrets" go even deeper. Daughters who were victims of physical or emotional abuse that their mothers were unwilling or unable to stop are likely to focus their unresolved pain and anger on their mothers. From deep within her, the grown daughter continues to cry out, "Where were you when I needed you? Why didn't you protect me?"

"I never even knew I blamed Mom for what my father did to me," Luanne explained. "I just knew I didn't like her very much. It wasn't until she and I finally talked about the abuse that I began to see her as a fellow sufferer rather than a traitor."

If you were the victim of abuse or molestation or incest, you may need to see a counselor who is qualified to help you work through your feelings of pain, loss, and abandonment.

Working It Out

Have you been harboring resentments against your mother? Do you have unanswered questions you need to ask her? Do you need to talk with her about family secrets? Now is the time to break down those barriers between you.

Remember: Neither you nor your mother can change the past. But you can work to understand each other now. You can try to clear up misperceptions or misunderstandings from the past.

If your mother lives close to you and you are able to see her alone frequently, begin to talk out difficult areas. Proceed slowly and gently; keep in mind that this may be difficult for her. And yet by discussing troubling incidents and by comparing how you and she remember them, you can start working out long-repressed, maybe even forgotten, feelings. You can begin the exciting project of tearing down those barriers.

Most mothers are sensitive to harsh criticism and accusations about the part they might have played in events that happened in the past. Think before you speak. Rehearse in your mind the issues you want to talk about with her. Plan non-threatening ways of approaching those issues.

Your goal should not be to beat her over the head with your feelings about the past; your goal should be to listen and understand each other. Comments like, "That was a terrible thing you did to me!" or "How could you have cared so little about my feelings?" not only will be unpleasant for your mother to hear, but they also will not help you in understanding each other.

You probably will find your mother concerned and cooperative if you describe your feelings with "I" words instead of accusing "you" words: "I was so scared when . . ." or "I was really angry when . . ." or "I was really worried when . . ." And remember to include in your memories words of sincere appreciation. You might say something such as, "I'm glad you're letting me tell you about this now. It really helps to talk to you."

If your mother doesn't live close to you, you can accomplish some of these same things by letter or telephone. But since neither is really a good substitute for talking face-to-face, for looking each other in the eye and hugging now and then, for maybe even shedding a tear or two, you probably should save the toughest topics for times you can be together.

STRATEGIES FOR HANDLING CONFLICT

You may be thinking, *Those are good ideas. Mom and I do have conflicts. But my question is, How do I go about handling them?*

I'm glad you asked! Here are some suggestions:

Be Ready to React in New Ways

Do certain comments, actions, or subjects set off you or your mother? If you think ahead and prepare how you will respond to those topics, you will be able to react in new, more appropriate ways. For instance, when your mother says for the thousandth time, "So, have you met a nice young man yet?" you have a choice: You can respond with your same old angry, "Give it a rest, Mom! Why can't you get off my back? I don't have to be married to be happy!"; or you can answer with a breezy, "No, but when and if I do, you can be sure you'll be the first to know!" If you have thought ahead about this topic, you can respond with your pre-planned comment and then move right into the new topic of conversation you have prepared just for this occasion.

This approach will allow you to switch from playing a defensive role to playing an offensive one. More important, you will have given your mom a wonderful message: We can disagree and still love and enjoy each other.

You Choose the Battles

Some issues are simply not worth fighting about. Not everything is important enough to take a stand on. Are there topics you would rather not discuss? That's your right. Are there subjects you definitely want to avoid? Let your mom know what they are. But at times you will need to choose to ignore or overlook minor irritations and focus instead on the major problem areas.

It's important to develop strategies that will help you avoid fights in which you would rather not get involved. One of these strategies is to answer lightly—or directly, if necessary—and then to change the subject. When your mom looks critically at your outfit and says, "You're going to ruin your arches wearing those high heels. And that skirt! Isn't it too short for someone your age?" you might respond with, "Let's not talk about my clothes today, Mom. You said you got a letter from Aunt Gladys. What did she have to say?"

Prepare Yourself for Visits

If you find the time you spend with your mom uncomfortable and difficult, here are some final suggestions for your visits with her:

Set a time limit. Instead of emphasizing how long you can stay with your mother, emphasize the quality of the time you will spend with her. Maybe it will be just lunch together. Or, if you have to travel to be with her, it may be an entire week. If you find it difficult to stay with her in her home, don't. Instead of moving back into your old room, you might stay with a friend or in a motel.

If your mother lives near you, you may find it harder to set limits on the time you spend together. But it can still be done. Try saying something such as: "I love you, Mom, and I enjoy being with you, but I need time for myself and my family. How about coming over for lunch on Friday?" This is so much better than saying, "Sure, Mom, stop in any time," and then boiling inside when she does.

Set ground rules, if necessary. If your mom won't stop criticizing your noisy dogs and the way you keep house, visit with her somewhere other than your home. Look for a neutral site—a shopping mall, perhaps, or a restaurant you both like. And if there are certain topics that always cause trouble ("So, when are you going to give me a grand-child?"), don't feel guilty about limiting the subjects about which you will talk ("Starting a family is such a private matter, Tom and I agreed not to talk about it to anyone but each other").

Plan your countermoves. One effective countermove is to call a "time-out" when things seem to be getting tense. ("The sun will be setting before long, Mom. Let's take a walk down along the beach and just enjoy the view.") Do it before things get so far along they can't be stopped without someone feeling hurt or cheated. You will be able to think of other countermoves of your own. But whichever ones you decide on, be positive in your approach. You will be setting the tone for your time together.

Change your expectations for your time together. See your time with your mom as a chance to grow closer rather than as something to be endured. Sure, problems will come up. Expect it and accept it. But, you know what? Each of those conflicts is a chance for you and your mother to understand each other a little bit more, a chance to learn to express your love and acceptance for each other in a more positive way. Be realistic, of course. But also expect the best.

Go ahead. Take the big step and throw out the old wornout script. Stop responding to each other with roles left over from your childhood. Write yourself some new lines. And when you act in new ways, your mom's script may change too.

Learn How to Handle Your Anger

For a long time, I thought that keeping my anger to myself was the best way to relate to my mother. When she offered unsolicited advice, I would simply smile and pretend to listen. When I visited my parents, I told myself that all I should hope for was to make the best of the situation.

We didn't do a very good job of expressing our anger in our family. Most of our feelings toward each other, whether they were feelings of anger or affection, generally went undemonstrated and unspoken.

But now that you are an adult, you can choose how you will handle your anger when you are with your mother. You can choose to remain in the old patterns, or you can choose more healthy ways of dealing with anger.

Express your anger before it reaches the boiling point. Sometimes it's so hard to say what we feel that we simply put off doing it. It's easy to assume that if we avoid dealing with a certain issue, the annoyance and frustration will somehow go away. Unfortunately, it seldom works that way. What actually happens is that things that started out small end up being misunderstood and blown out of proportion because we don't talk about them.

This doesn't mean you need to vent every little irritation. But when you let the anger and frustration build up to where you pass the point of no return, you are certain to overreact. Instead of expressing yourself clearly and calmly, you probably will blow up and say things you'll later regret. Your reason for keeping quiet in the first place was to create more closeness and prevent friction between you and your mom. But when you ignore or stifle your anger, you end may up destroying whatever closeness you had.

The answer is to deal with your feelings before you reach the boiling point. If something is bothering you, talk about it. Often this can be done gently, even painlessly. You might say something such as, "Mom, it seems as if every time I see you, you ask me how much I weigh. That really bothers me. I'm watching my diet, but it's something I don't want to discuss. Okay?" If she brings up the subject again, you can say—kindly but firmly, "Remember? We aren't going to talk about my weight." Then change the subject.

Learn How to Handle Manipulation

One of the difficulties you may encounter when you begin to work on your relationship to your mother is her ability to manipulate you. If you feel she is manipulative, the two of you need to talk about it. As Ephesians 4:15 instructs, you need to "speak . . . the truth in love."

If you have a lifetime history of always giving in to your mother, don't be surprised when she continues to expect you to give in. Her manipulation will keep on as long as you allow it to do so. The thing to keep in mind is that no one can manipulate you unless you allow it. Manipulation isn't something that's done *to* you, it's something done *with* you.

Manipulation is a habit—a bad habit. But even bad habits can be broken.

Some manipulative mothers are amazingly adept at their job. They know how to pile on ever greater pressures. If that doesn't work, they bring in the heavy artillery. They use silence ("If you won't be reasonable, there's no use discussing it"), bribes ("You've got to come. I bought you a really special present, and it's too fragile to mail"), rewards ("I was thinking about your broken-down washing machine. After you say yes to this one little request, I'll buy you a new one"). It takes strength and determination to resist such tactics.

If you are struggling to break the cycle of manipulation, remember these six things:

More than anyone else, your mother knows how to get to you. That's not so surprising when you consider the years she's had to watch and learn. The question is, Are you going to let her get to you?

When some mothers can't get their way, they needle and taunt. Some mothers, in fact, go so far as to ridicule, belittle, and really hurt. At such times, you may need to say, "Mom, I know you want me to call you every morning, but your needling me about it all the time only makes me more resistant to you."

You can ignore your mother's bait. "Someday *you'll* be old," she says. "Then you'll know what it feels like." Or, "When I'm gone, you'll wish you had done this one little thing for me." Or, "Why can't you be like your sister? She really cares about me." Sure she's baiting you. But, remember, you can't be manipulated unless you cooperate. As long as she knows how to get a particular reaction out of you, she will be able to manipulate you. If you don't respond to her manipulation, she loses her power. Suddenly, you're the one in control. Accept her bait or ignore it. It's up to you.

Don't retaliate by manipulating her. Your goal is not to turn things around to where you can be the one doing the manipulating. Remember that your goal is to gain a new and better way of relating to your mom and her to you.

Anticipate your mother's recriminations. Especially anticipate those aimed at making you feel guilty. Refuse to accept the guilt. If your mother has standard lines such as, "After all I've sacrificed for you, I never thought you'd begrudge me this one little thing," have some appropriate responses ready. You might say, "I appreciate all you've done, Mom. I know you've sacrificed a lot. Now I hope you'll try to understand how I feel about this."

Prayer changes things. It really does! When your mother seems to push you beyond your limits, ask the Lord to give you wisdom about what to say to her. Ask God to help you resist the temptation to "conform to the evil desires you had when you lived in ignorance" and instead to help you to "conform to the likeness of his Son" (1 Peter 1:14; Rom. 8:29). With wisdom and strength from the Lord, you can reach that new plane you are seeking with your mother.

Again, change doesn't come overnight. The conflicts between the two of you have developed and grown over a period of many years. But if you prayerfully think about what is happening between you and plan your actions as well as your responses to her actions, you can greatly reduce the conflict areas in your relationship.

Learn How to Handle Criticism

When Mom says for the fiftieth time, "It's raining. Why didn't you wear your boots?" you have a choice: Will you hear her criticizing your lack of good sense, or will you hear her genuine concern about your well-being? Answering with, "I usually do, although I did forget today," is one way of responding to her concern for you. It ignores the possibility that she may in fact be criticizing your foolishness—or that she has an irritating habit of interfering in your life.

You'll know you are really independent when you are able to accept your mother's criticism as expressions of her love and concern for you.

7.

Making Peace with Your Mother

You have already examined the way in which you and your mother respond to conflict. And you have discovered ways in which you can change your response to her. You're off to a good start! Now you need to take some deliberate steps toward making peace with her. I'm not talking about changing her, remember. I'm talking about finding out, and coming to understand, just who she is. When you really know her and understand her, it will be much easier for you to begin to accept who she is and why she does the things she does.

ACCEPT YOUR MOTHER

The more you understand your mother, the more you will be able to accept her. The more you can accept her, the closer you will feel to her. The closer you feel to her, the stronger your loving friendship will grow. But it all starts with understanding.

Understand Your Mother's Behavior

Do you need help understanding your mom? Think back to your childhood. How did you perceive her then, and how do you perceive her now? Perhaps the following questions will help point you in the right direction.

How open was your mother about her feelings? When you were growing up, did she talk about the things that made her sad? Did she tell you what frightened her or made her angry or caused her to feel helpless? Did she let down her barriers and show you she was vulnerable? How does she handle her feelings now?

Did she help you feel free to express your feelings? When you were a child, could you let your feelings show, or were you expected to keep them to yourself? When you cried, were you told to "stop acting like a baby," or were you cuddled and comforted? When you were hurt or frightened or angry, did your mother recognize and acknowledge those emotions, or did she respond with platitudes ("Every cloud has a silver lining")? Did she minimize your feelings ("If you think you have problems now, just wait until you have to deal with real life")? Did she threaten you ("Keep up that crying, and I'll give you something to really cry about!")? Does she help you feel free to express your feelings now?

Did your mother let you know you were loved? Did she tell you she loved you? Did she convey to you that you were lovable even when your behavior was not? Did you grow up feeling loved and cared for? What specifically did your mother do to express and show her affection for you? How does she express her love for you now?

Did your mother really listen to what you had to say? Did she take joy in hearing you, or was her listening tinged with impatience, criticism, or judgment? Did she encourage you to talk with her? We all want to be listened to, but if disapproval is the price of being heard, we may decide it's better to keep quiet.

Learn About Your Mother's Background

When my husband, Larry, and I were first married, he was stationed with the Air Force in Arkansas. My parents were raised in the Ozark Mountains in southern Missouri, and we still had a lot of relatives living there. For the first time in my life, I had a chance to meet relatives and childhood friends of my mother. It was in Missouri that I really started to know my mom.

You might want to spend some time researching your mother's family background. Meet her friends and relatives who knew her when she was young or when she was a young mother. Ask questions and listen to stories. Look at old pictures. By coming to see the family legacy that was handed down to her, you just might learn to identify some forces that are beyond her control.

Judith grew up with a mother who expressed almost no love for Judith and her two brothers. Judith's mother met her children's physical needs, but the affection just wasn't there. "I didn't want to be that kind of mother to my own children," Judith said. "But I was afraid I was destined to be. That was my mother; that would be me."

Just before Judith's first child was born, she finally had an opportunity to meet and talk with her mother's relatives. Only then did she find out the reason for her mother's coldness.

"I had an older sister, something I never knew," Judith explained. "My mother loved her so much! But just weeks before the baby's second birthday, she died suddenly of meningitis. My mother was heartbroken. She was convinced God had taken her baby away from her because she loved the child too much. When my brothers and I came along, Mother was afraid to love us so intensely. So, though she cared deeply for us, she was careful not to show it. In my mother's mind, withholding her love was a demonstration of just how much she truly did care."

When her mother came to visit after the birth of

Judith's baby girl, Judith asked her mother about the chid she had lost. For the first time in her life, Judith listened as her mother poured out expressions of the love and concern she had kept carefully tucked away for so many years. For the first time ever, mother and daughter wept together.

Finally, Judith began to understand her mother's motivations. With understanding came forgiveness. With forgiveness came acceptance. With acceptance came the love from and for her mother—love for which Judith had longed her entire life.

Break the Pattern

Judith is the loving, affectionate mother she longed to be. She broke out of the pattern her mother had cast for her. You can do the same. Isn't that good news? Keep these things in mind when you set about to break the pattern:

Accept what you can. I know, I know. Sometimes you're tempted just to chuck the whole idea of working with your mom. But don't do it. Her positive side is there. You may need to look for it, but it will be worth the effort.

Reject what you must. You surely will find in your mom some things you will need to reject. But don't toss out too much too quickly. Be prayerfully selective. And remember, reject behavior or attitudes, not the person.

Give in on some things. Did I hear you groan and mutter at this suggestion? Now, hold on a minute. Just think about it. Surely some things that are not all that important to you are very important to your mother. What would it hurt to give in on these? When Mom greets you at the door with, "Have you written to Aunt Florence recently? She always asks about you. She would really love to hear from you," it might be one of those times. Now, you may think that you have nothing to write to an aunt you never see and don't even know, but if it's important to your mother, isn't it worth the few minutes it would take to compose a short note?

If your mother sometimes needs you to show your love for her on her own terms, give her that. Giving in now and then doesn't weaken your position. On the contrary, it strengthens it.

Stay open. As you break free of old patterns, be ready for some surprises. For instance, you may believe that the critical attitude your mother passed along to you is responsible for the difficulty you are having making friends. You successfully change your attitude only to find that you still have friendship problems. Recognizing and changing old patterns will not solve all your problems. And it won't settle all the conflicts and answer all the questions you may be facing. You may actually find that your mother wasn't the cause of as many of your problems as you had always assumed.

Be patient. Worthwhile changes rarely come quickly or easily. They take time and work and ever so much patience. When you become discouraged, think of how good it will feel when you can look into your mother's eyes and honestly say, "You're my friend!"

LEARN TO COMMUNICATE WITH YOUR MOTHER

If you ever hope to improve your relationship to your mother, you must first learn to communicate with her. And if you really want to communicate with her, you must learn to generate a more receptive atmosphere, rather than an antagonistic one. That means you've got to make a real effort to stop judging her, criticizing her, and tuning her out. Unless you listen open-mindedly to her, how can you ever expect her to listen receptively to you?

Responsive Listening

You'll find that responsive listening can do a lot to improve your relationship to your mom. Most of us learned poor communication skills when we were young, especially when it came to understanding and expressing our feelings. With such a background, we often continue to send to each other messages that are vague, ambiguous, and contradictory.

How are you in this area? If you need some work, try paying attention to your listening habits with your mom. Do you interrupt her? Do you feel that most of what she says is too inconsequential to be worth your time? Do you find your mind wandering while she's talking? If you look hard enough, you will almost certainly be able to discover a number of ways to break through the communication barriers between you and your mother.

To start, practice responsive listening. This type of listening is made up of three main steps: (1) understand the other person's perspective, (2) admit you're not always right, and (3) stay even-tempered and patient throughout the process. Here's how they could apply to you and your mother.

Understand Your Mother's Perspective

Try to listen to your mother in a way that will allow you to understand the feelings that lie beneath her words. Try to listen with the goal of sharing her frame of reference.

Rather than blame her for the past or attack her for her opinions, search her words for the experiences, attitudes, and emotions that are hidden underneath. For instance, when you feel like shouting, "How can you say such a foolish thing? You're so hopelessly out of touch!" try instead to determine why she feels the way she does. You may discover that if you had had her background, if you had been raised as she was raised, if you had had her parents and lived in her time, you just might be saying and feeling the same things she is saying and feeling.

When you come to the place where you can honestly tell your mother, "I understand how you feel," it will be a good indication that you are listening to her in an understanding way. If you are a mother yourself, you can put yourself in her shoes. It's easy for you to accuse her of making bad decisions, but what about the decisions you make regarding your children? Do they always seem fair, wise, and attractive to your children? Are you always clear-headed and in control when you make decisions? Putting yourself in your mother's shoes will help you understand her perspective.

Understanding where your mom is coming from doesn't mean you have to agree with her every opinion about the way you should conduct your life. But it does mean that she can safely express her feelings to you. Once she knows you can understand and appreciate her point of view, it just may be that she will feel less driven to impose her opinions on you.

Whenever you feel yourself becoming impatient with your mom or judgmental or critical of her proclamations and opinions, stop for a moment. Step back and consider how you would feel if you were in her place. Instead of resisting her, do what you can to understand her. Ask questions. Demonstrate your interest. Encourage your mother to help you understand how and why she feels and acts the way she does. Philippians 2:4 tells us: "Look not only to your own interests, but also to the interests of others." Be interested in your mother's frame of reference.

Admit You're Not Always Right

You're not, you know. None of us is. When you insist, "I'm right and you're wrong," your mother will feel required to defend herself by saying, "No, *I'm* right and *you're* wrong!" Responsive listening allows you to hear the matter from her perspective. She needs to know that you appreciate her freedom to have her own point of view. By insisting your feelings are always right, you're in effect saying that unless she feels the same way you do, her feelings are wrong.

One of the hardest and most important aspects of a loving, close relationship is being able to value and accept very different points of view. Again, this doesn't mean you have to agree with everything your mom says. And you should not pretend you do. But you can begin your comments with such phrases as: "I can see . . ." or "I understand . . ." or "I appreciate your saying . . ." If you adopt an attitude of acceptance, your mother will be much more likely to try to understand and accept your point of view as well.

Stay Even-tempered

The third step in responsive listening may be the hardest for you: stay patient and even-tempered. If you feel as if you want to jump at your mother at every chance, if you feel as if you can't bear to listen to one more of her reruns about Aunt Sue, then try these suggestions:

Listen for the truth in what she says. If your mother criticizes the way you do things, try to listen to her as objectively as you possibly can. You needn't do everything her way, but perhaps you shouldn't be so quick to reject it all either. For example, when your mother warns you to wear boots in the rain or you'll get your shoes wet and catch a cold, it just could be that you really *don't* generally wear boots in the rain, and your shoes really *do* get soaked, and you often *do* end up with a cold. Perhaps your mother's comments are constructive ones that you ought to listen to. If, on the other hand, your feet don't get that wet and you almost never have a cold, you can simply thank her for her concern and tell her it's not a problem to you.

Learn to say "I love you" first. Be the first to say "I love you." For some daughters, these words come only with great difficulty. That may be the case for you as well. Still, it's up to you to be the first to speak them. If you wait for your mom to speak first, the words may never come at all.

Practice saying "I love you" often. Say it even when it's not what your mother wants to hear. For instance, when she pressures you to spend an evening with her and you have other plans, you might say, "I love you, Mom, but I can't come over tonight. We'll set aside an evening next week."

MAKING PEACE WITH YOUR MOTHER

You may be thinking, *Making peace with my mother sounds fine, but you don't know my mother. I have so much anger built up against her. What can I do?*

Good question. Here are some suggestions for making peace in a constructive way:

Make a List of Your Resentments

Write down each painful memory you carry, each bitter recollection you harbor. Make your list as specific as you possibly can. As you are listing your hurts and resentments, you may feel a number of other feelings as well. That's all right. It's only in dealing with those feelings that you can hope to get your anger or hurt or bitterness out of your system.

But keep one thing firmly in mind: Your purpose is not to dredge up every old hurt or to punish your mother for the past. Your goal is to help heal childhood wounds and so to make whole your capacity to love and understand your mother. Therefore, *under no circumstances* should you show your list to your mother. It is for you, not for her.

Imagine Yourself Reading Your List Aloud to Your Mother

Picture your mother listening to you as you read. See her lovingly acknowledge your hurt and anger. Imagine her understanding exactly how you feel. Hear her say, "I'm so glad you are finally telling me your feelings. Please continue. Let out all your hurt." Although this is happening only in your imagination, do your best to feel yourself being understood, loved, and comforted by your mother. You will be surprised at what a powerful healing effect this imagined exchange can have.

When you have finished imagining, spend some time praying. Tell the Lord how badly you want an end to the anger and bitterness you have harbored so long. Ask his guidance in your dealings with your mother.

Share Your Feelings with Someone Close to You

You don't want to make things worse by dumping your resentments on your mother. But you do need the understanding support of someone who truly cares about you.

You may choose a close friend, your husband, a brother or sister. Be sure it's someone you trust, someone who's willing to listen to what can be a painful and emotional time of sharing. You aren't asking that person for advice, and certainly not for criticism or judgment. You just want him or her to listen.

With you and your helper sitting face-to-face, read your list of resentments aloud. It may be a hard thing to do. You may feel embarrassed about sharing such intense feelings. You may feel guilty for feeling the way you do. In fact, it may be a good idea to warn your friend ahead of time that this might not be an easy thing for you, but that it's nevertheless important that you get through it.

When you're finished, tell your friend what you most would like to hear from your mother just now. A request for forgiveness? Explanations? Sincere expressions of her love and caring? Then try to imagine your mother saying just what you need to hear.

All that was background work. You'll notice that none of it really involved your mother at all. It was just for you. After all, it's you you're working on. Here are a couple more suggestions. They will take a bit more effort:

Imagine Yourself in a Room with Both Your Mother and Christ

With Christ as a silent listener at first, read your list of resentments to your mother. Now visualize Christ's response. What does he do? What does he say to the two of you? What is your response to his presence?

Forgive Your Mother

Oscar Wilde once said, "Children begin by loving their parents; as they grow older they judge them; sometimes they forgive them."* Now is the time for forgiveness.

Maybe you *didn't* get the mothering you needed. Maybe your mother hasn't treated you as she ought to have. Maybe she really is obstinate and stubborn and hard to get along with. That just shows that you, like the rest of us, are the daughter of an imperfect mother.

Mothers make mistakes. Some mothers make big ones. If you have children, you'll make mistakes with them too— if you haven't already. Chances are, your kids will have complaints about you. When that happens, won't you be glad you set an example of forgiveness?

To forgive doesn't mean to forget. To forgive doesn't mean to whitewash all the disputes and differences you and your mother have had over the years. To forgive does mean

*Picture of Dorian Gray, 1891.

you need to let go of your hurts, to change your attitude from one of resentment and distrust to one of love.

You may ask, But *how* do I forgive? Forgiveness is a decision of the will, not a feeling. You can decide to forgive even if you don't feel like forgiving.

Let me make a suggestion. Take the list of your resentments against your mother, and make it a part of your daily devotional time. Pray about each resentment, one at a time. Offer it to Christ. Tell him of your desire to forgive your mother for whatever it is you resent. If you don't feel that you can honestly pray that you want to forgive her, ask Christ to make you "willing to be made willing."

Don't feel a need to rush the process. You may want to pray about one resentment for several days or even weeks. Then allow Christ's healing power to touch each area of resentment. As you offer each one to him, say, "Lord, I give you my _____ (name feeling) toward my mother for _____ (name resentment). I don't want it anymore. I choose to forgive her for _____. Help me through this decision of my will to feel as if I have forgiven her. Heal me of these resentments and broken areas."

Then trust Christ to do his transforming work in you and in your relationship with your mother.

As time passes and as you begin to sense some of the resentment lift, write a letter to your mom (a letter you will never mail). Write a statement of forgiveness about each resentment on your list. Allow the letter—which may be written over a fairly long period of time—to be your tangible evidence of the Lord's healing in your relationship.

Isn't it good to know you can disagree with your mother and still love her? Isn't it a great feeling to be able to express your anger or your sadness and not feel you are alienating her for life? Isn't it wonderful to look at the differences between the two of you and find that you can actually respect and appreciate them, that you can even learn from them?

You may find it will take a while for your feelings of forgiveness to catch up with your decision to forgive. Don't worry. If your wounds are deep, inflicted over many years, the feeling of forgiveness won't come easily. You will have to trust God for it. Surely he, who commanded you to forgive, will enable you to do so.

8.

Making Friends
with Your Mother

You thought about the reasons why your relationship is the way it is. You have looked at ways of trying to break free from your mother. You have explored the areas of conflict and have examined methods for making peace. Now it's time to move a step further. It's time to actually make friends with your mother.

Handling conflict means finding ways to avert arguments and battles with your mom. Making peace means laying those battles aside. Making friends means coming to the place where you truly enjoy being with her.

Rosemary is a beautiful woman in her mid-thirties. Tall and willowy, she strikes an imposing figure that would bring pride to the heart of any mother. Well, not *any* mother.

"My mom can't accept the fact that I'm still single," Rosemary says. "And she's mortified that I'm a house painter. Never mind that I make an excellent living with my business and employ three other people. I'm not a teacher or a secretary or a nurse. I'm not married with 2.3 children, so I'm a disappointment to her."

"I'm forty-two years old," says Donna. "I have a great job. My dentist husband and I have been happily married for almost fifteen years. My children are great; everyone comments on what good kids they are. So why do I feel like such a failure when I'm around my mother?"

Age doesn't magically confer on you the ability to get

along with your mother. The battles that began in your adolescent years don't, even with time, automatically give way to a blissful peace—or even to an uneasy truce. That's not news, is it?

You want to make friends with your mother. You want to sit with her and sip coffee and talk about mutual interests and enjoy each other. That's probably what she wants too. So how do you go about making friends with your mother?

WHAT IS FRIENDSHIP?

Think of your closest, dearest friends. What are the qualities that you value in them? Is it the acceptance you get from them? Is it the open sharing that goes on between you? Is it the listening? Or the mutual support?

It is unrealistic to expect from your mother the same things you have come to expect from your best friends. After all, she's different from them. And your friendship with her will most likely be different from your friendships with other people.

WHAT IS UNIQUE ABOUT A FRIENDSHIP WITH YOUR MOTHER?

First, you have *chosen* many of your friends. You were attracted to them (and they to you) for a variety of reasons, and you decided to pursue the relationship. However, you didn't choose your mother. Your relationship to her is a given. What you can choose, though, is the quality of that relationship. You can choose whether or not you will make that relationship into a friendship.

"But you don't know my mother," you may be saying. "She's incapable of being the kind of friend I need." That may be true. She may not be able to share openly with you or give mutual support or listen attentively. But you can take the first step on the road to friendship by modeling those qualities to her. You can "do to her what you would want her to do to you." Demonstrate responsive listening to her. Affirm her. Express acceptance of ways in which she is different from you. And be careful to let your actions be motivated by love, not by a hidden agenda to change her into something she's not.

The second unique quality about a friendship with your mother comes from the Bible. Again and again Scripture admonishes us to *honor* our fathers and mothers.

Honor Your Mother

What does the word *honor* mean in the context of your relationship to your mother? Does it mean you never disagree with her? Does it mean you must meet her every expectation of you? Does it mean you must obey her forever? The answer to all these questions is no. To be bound to agree with your mother about everything, to be obliged to conform to her expectations, to face a lifetime of childish obedience to her would produce a relationship that is the exact opposite of friendship.

So what *does* it mean to honor your mother? Let's look at how Scripture defines *honor*.

Prize your mother highly. The writer of Proverbs tells us: "Esteem her [wisdom], and she will exalt you; embrace her, and she will honor you" (Prov. 4:8). In this verse, the word "honor" indicates the idea of being raised into an exalted position, of being highly prized.

Simply because your mother gave you life, she deserves to be highly prized. And surely you can think of other things for which she deserves to be exalted, lifted up, honored. Think about the sacrifices she has made for you, not in a guilt-producing way but in an honoring way. What has she given up for your benefit? Or think about the things she has taught you—to knit, to cook, to love good music, to paint a fence, to grow roses, to be a faithful spouse. Did she teach you to love God? Prize her highly for these contributions she has made to your life.

Take time to make a list of the specific things for which you highly prize your mom. When it is appropriate, express your honor to your mom by telling her that you recognize and value highly what she has done for you. Articulating your honor to her not only will encourage her, but it also will strengthen you as you hear yourself saying these affirming things to your mom.

Care for your mother. A verse from the Psalms gives another clue about how you can honor your mother: "He will call upon me, and I will deliver him; I will be with him in trouble, I will deliver him and honor him" (Ps. 91:15). To honor your mother means to care for her, to be there when she needs you, to assist her and help her.

Has your mom had physical needs you were able to meet? Has she needed you to be with her at times? Has she needed emotional support during difficult times in her life? How have you responded? By caring for your mom, you are obeying the biblical injunction to honor her.

Show respect for your mother. In the Old Testament books of the law, we read, "Each of you is to respect his mother and father" (Lev. 19:3a). Yes, that's what the Bible says. You are to respect your mom. You don't respect her, you say? Perhaps you need to look at her with fresh eyes ready to find the qualities worthy of admiration.

Although Teresa's mother was mentally slow, she successfully raised four happy, healthy children. Teresa, exceptionally bright, was embarrassed by her mother. When Teresa married and had children of her own, she always talked about her mother in a negative way. One day Teresa was shocked to hear her eight-year-old son tell a neighbor that his grandmother was "a nut case, a real loony tune."

Have you at times been disrespectful of your mother?

Have you insulted her or mocked her, perhaps even ridiculed her? One major consequence of repeatedly showing disrespect is that disrespect breeds disdain, and disdain breeds contempt.

If you can identify ways in which you have shown disrespect or felt disrespectful toward your mother, confess them to God. Ask for his forgiveness and for his strength to replace your disrespect with respect. Then take some time to make a list of qualities in her that you honestly can respect. When you have the opportunity, *show* her that respect. Thank her for demonstrating those qualities to you. Tell her how they have positively affected your own life.

One wonderful consequence of showing respect is that it breeds respect. And respect breeds friendship.

Obey your mother. The New Testament tells us, "Children, obey your parents in the Lord, for this is right" (Eph. 6:1). Without a doubt, obedience can be part of honor. This important commandment, however, is given to children, not adults.

In your mother's eyes, you may forever be her little girl, forever bound to obey her. But the fact is that you are no longer a child; you are now an adult. As an adult it is up to you to make your own decisions, then to accept any consequences for those decisions.

For instance, your mother might say, "You should never send your family out in the morning without a good hot breakfast. You need to go to bed at a decent hour so you don't have so much trouble getting up in the morning." Now it just may be that your family doesn't want bacon and eggs in the morning or stewed prunes and oatmeal for breakfast. And it may be that your evening hours are far more productive for you than your morning hours. Must you change your routine simply because your mother tells you to?

Absolutely not. You can say to your mother, "Thanks for your concern, Mom, but this is what works best for us."

As a grown daughter, you are to prize your mother, to care for her, and to show her respect. But obedience is no longer required of you.

Perhaps you feel you can't truly prize your mother. You may doubt your ability to care for her. You may feel very little respect for her. I've got good news for you! God will help you. Through his grace, you *can* learn to prize your mother, care for her, and respect her. You can learn to honor your mother.

MOVE TOWARD FRIENDSHIP

Perhaps your relationship to your mother already is established on mutual respect. Perhaps you already have come to the point where you truly do appreciate each other. Perhaps you already admire each other. If so, you already have a good foundation in place. If not, these suggestions may give you further guidelines in building a stronger foundation.

Respect Your Differences

Recognize the fact that you and your mom are different people. Certainly your ages separate you, and maybe your life experiences do too. And the ways in which you were raised may be totally different. Maybe you are also divided by your religious convictions. And maybe you differ on certain life values. But that's where mutual respect comes in. As two adults, you can understand and accept that having differences doesn't mean something is wrong. It just means you are different people.

Feeling free to express yourself even when you know your mom doesn't share your ideas is a wonderfully comfortable feeling. The same is true for your mother. When you agree to disagree sometimes and not feel threatened about it, you can truly feel acceptable to, and accepting of, your mother.

Take the Initiative

Putting it bluntly, one mother said, "I know I'm not perfect. But I'm sixty-two years old, and I'm not going to change." So your mom isn't likely to change. That's all right. You can do a lot yourself. If you take the initiative, you may be pleasantly surprised to see how eager your mother is to join in. You may want to try these things:

Set up time to be together. You don't have to plan anything in particular, just do something you both can enjoy. Have lunch together, for instance. Or spend some time together in the garden. Or watch a television program together. Or bake pies. The important thing is to set up time when you can concentrate on being together and enjoy it.

Call her on the telephone. You may have many other things going on in your life, but your mother may not. It's important for her to hear your voice, to know you are interested in her. By taking the initiative in communicating with her, you are letting your mom know you want to improve your relationship for her benefit as well as yours.

Send her notes in the mail. Sure, you send her birthday and Mother's Day cards, but what about notes just to say you care about her? How about a card with a special message that fits her particularly well? The possibilities are endless. The point is to let your mother know you are eager to build a better, stronger relationship between the two of you. If you take the initiative in expressing your love to your mother in ways that are meaningful to her, you may find you will need to spend a lot less time responding to and reacting to her.

Communicate Lovingly

Do you have trouble finding things about which you and your mother can safely talk? Why not make a list of all the things about which the two of you agree. Try to find at least five topics that won't cause you problems. Then, when things get off onto sticky subjects, call up your list and switch to a safe one.

You say your mother is one of those people who insists on bringing up problem subjects? Try to reframe your differences ("I know how you feel about my being single, Mom, but I hope you can understand that . . ."). Then immediately switch over to another subject ("All this talk about marriage reminds me of your old wedding album. Can we get it out and look at it?").

Show Interest in Your Mother

One of the nicest ways to begin to relate to your mother is to ask her about herself. Most daughters never hear their mothers' stories—usually because the daughters never ask. You also might try to remember an event that had an impact on you and ask your mother how she remembers it. I asked my mother about the first of the foster children who lived with us, about my kitten that walked home across the Golden Gate Bridge, and about the time the Christmas money was stolen out of her purse. In every case, her memory of the incident was different from mine.

Show interest in your mom by allowing her to be involved in your life. Tell her about important events and people in your life. Have her meet your friends. If you have children, ask her to join you for excursions with the kids. Share good books with her. Ask for her opinion once in a while. If this is difficult for you, you might want to try asking her questions and opinions that are not too open-ended. "Do you think I should buy the blue dress or wear my green one?" might be safer than "What do you think I should wear?"

And let your mother be useful in your life. It's important to your mother to be able to be helpful to you. Let her. Sure you need to be independent, but would it hurt to need her in a *few* areas? Ask her for recipes. Let her help you with mending or sewing or gardening. Let her take out your children, if she wants to give you time for yourself.

Choose to See the Good

In Philippians 4:8 the apostle Paul tells us: "Whatsoever things are true, whatsoever things are noble, whatsoever things are just, whatsoever things are pure, whatsoever things are lovely, whatsoever things are of good report, if there be any virtue and if there is anything praiseworthy—meditate on these things" (NIV).

When you are barraged by negative memories, you may need to exercise some discipline. Bad recollections have a habit of jumping up and attacking at the worst possible times. Before you know it, you may have blurted them out. The outcome is sure to be an atmosphere of discord.

Instead of dwelling on the negative memories, choose to think about the positive ones. Or create new memories. Brooding over past injustices leaves us with little emotion with which to create a better future.

When you are tempted to blame your mother for problem areas in your life, choose instead to take responsibility for your own actions. It is far more profitable to use your energy in admitting and learning from the wrong choices you may have made than in trying to blame your mother for what has happened to you. It may feel good to blame your mom, but it probably is not the just and true thing to do.

Or when you are so aware of your mother's flaws that you can't enjoy her company, choose to think about her strong qualities. "If there is *anything* praiseworthy," think about it. That doesn't mean you act as if she has no flaws. You can appreciate her virtues without denying her flaws. It's a matter of choice and focus. Will you focus on the flaws, or will you focus on what is virtuous, what is praiseworthy?

The New Testament instructs us to "Be kind and compassionate to one another, forgiving each other, just as in Christ God forgave you" (Eph. 4:32). When you consider your mother, be compassionate. If she has made lots of mistakes as a mother, choose to see her intentions rather than her actions. Try to understand that she did the best she could under the circumstances in which she was operating. If you are a mother yourself, you need look only to your own life as a mother to realize that mothers aren't perfect. Don't be hard on her, and try to forgive her for her shortcomings. Choose to focus on what is good.

Hang in There

You say you're discouraged? You say you aren't getting any cooperation? You say you're not seeing any results? Well, please don't quit. It's too soon to give up. As long as you and your mother are both alive, keep working at your relationship.

If the bond between the two of you wasn't so powerful and important, this whole process wouldn't be nearly so difficult. You wouldn't care so much.

Even if your attempts so far have seemed dismal failures, even if those high hopes you started out with have all turned to bitter disappointment, *don't quit yet!* Gather up your ego, go back and try again. Don't wait for it all to work out. You *make* it work. You and your mom *can* be good friends. It's worth the struggle!

9.

Making Friends with a Non-Christian Mother

"My mother is a great woman," Ruthanne told me. "She raised me to be honest and to respect authority and to be a faithful and loving wife and mother. When I was growing up, all my friends envied me. They always said, 'What a great mom you have!' Well, I did have a great mom, and I still do. The only thing is, she doesn't know the Lord."

"My mom's philosophy of life was, 'Get them before they get you,'" Peggy said. "It was always us against the system. When I got older, it was my mom against me. Now it's my mom against everyone. To her, God is nothing but a swearword."

When a Christian daughter is working toward a friendship with her believing mother, the two are building on a common foundation. They have the advantage of starting from a unified point. But when a Christian daughter is working toward a friendship with a non-Christian mother, the two are coming from entirely different starting points. Whether a non-believing mother is "ideal" like Ruthanne's or hostile like Peggy's, she comes to the mother-daughter relationship from a frame of reference very different from that of her Christian daughter.

SCRIPTURAL PRINCIPLES

The Bible doesn't directly address every situation we face in our lives. For instance, it doesn't give clear instructions about how a Christian daughter should relate to her non-Christian mother. Yet this doesn't mean we are left to flounder about without any guidelines. The Scripture does give us basic principles from which to operate.

Actions Speak Louder Than Words

In the New Testament we read Peter's instructions to wives of unbelieving husbands. Although your relationship to your mother is quite different from the relationship between a husband and wife, I think you'll agree that some of the same principles apply to both situations. What direction can you find in these verses for daughters of non-Christian mothers?

> Wives, in the same way be submissive to your husbands so that, if any of them do not believe the word, they be won over without words by the behavior of their wives, when they see the purity and reverence of their lives. Your beauty should not come from outward adornment, such as braided hair and the wearing of gold jewelry and fine clothes. Instead, it should be that of your inner self, the unfading beauty of a gentle and quiet spirit, which is of great worth in God's sight (1 Peter 3:1–4).

In any relationship between a Christian and a non-Christian, it's up to the Christian to demonstrate what it means to be a child of God. Your mother may neither know nor care about what God says, but she does care about you. She will watch your actions, and she will listen to your words, at least for a time.

"I look for every possible chance to tell my mother about the Lord," says Ruthanne. "I tell her I love her too much to be separated from her for all eternity. I look for every opportunity to quote Scripture to her. I point out that she is a sinner and that the wages of sin is death. And I warn her about the consequences of rejecting God's gift of eternal life."

How successful is Ruthanne? "Mom used to discuss and debate with me. Now she either pointedly changes the subject, or she just tunes me out."

Lecturing seldom works. Preaching and nagging and condemning are even less likely to be successful. Not that this is surprising. Didn't you always hate being lectured to or preached at or nagged or condemned by your mom? So why would it be any different for her?

A much better approach is to let your mom—the one who probably knows you better than just about anyone in the world—see you in action. Demonstrate your gentle and quiet spirit to her. Let her be won over by your behavior.

As a disciple of Jesus, you have the blessed responsibility of being a witness of Christ's love and power to your mother. It just may be that your consistent actions will be the door to her openness to the Lord.

On the one hand, having the opportunity to reveal Christ's nature to your mother is a joy, but on the other hand it's also a fairly heavy responsibility that is added to your friendship. And it's a responsibility you can't carry alone.

Pray for God to work through you. You will need to commit yourself to consistent prayer for your relationship. When you are with your mother, you may find yourself acting in very un-Christian ways, especially if your mother has the ability to bring out the worst in you. You will need to prepare for your time together by praying that God's spirit will keep you from saying and doing things that are inconsistent with his character. Ask him to use you as his spokesperson to your mother.

Enlist the help of your Christian friends. Ask them to pray for you when you know you will be seeing or talking with your mom. You will need their support, especially if your mother is hostile about your Christian faith. You will need them to come alongside you and listen to you when she may have hurt you with harsh and condemning words. They will need to express their understanding when your mother can't begin to understand why you spend time at a Bible study or why you give money to your church or why you won't let your teenager see R-rated movies. You need the undergirding strength of believers who know what it costs you to reflect Christ to your mother.

Sometimes you even may need their admonition. Could it be you are putting too much pressure on your mother? You may not think so, but then it's very hard for you to be truly objective. Are you judging her too harshly? You may need a view that is more dispassionate than your own.

RESERVE JUDGMENT

Donnalee was driving her mother to a doctor's appointment when a squirrel suddenly darted out in front of her car. She swerved, but the crunch beneath her tire was unmistakable. Tears sprang to Donnalee's eyes. She slammed on the brakes and jumped from the car to see if there was anything she could do to help the tiny creature. There wasn't. When she got back in the car, tears were streaming down her cheeks.

"Oh, for heaven's sake, Donnalee," her mother chided. "It's only a squirrel!"

When Donnalee told me this story, she ended by saying, "That's how it is with a non-Christian mother. She just can't show sympathy for God's creation."

We insist that we prize individuality, that we cherish the differences God created in us. Yet in actuality, we tend to value and cherish in other people the characteristics that are most similar to our own. Donnalee is a sensitive person. Her mother, on the other hand, is more pragmatic and matter-of-fact. Would she have responded differently if she had been a Christian? Not necessarily.

As Christians, we often are too quick to make value judgments about what we believe is *the* Christian attitude.

In reality, the differences you see between you and your mother may be due merely to a difference in your temperaments. It's very important not to look at your non-Christian mother and interpret every characteristic or action as an indication of her lack of a personal relationship to God.

You know something? Christian mothers get tired and frustrated too. They argue with their daughters, and they sometimes are unreasonable. Sometimes they are unfeeling, unsympathetic, and critical. Christian mothers are just as human and just as fraught with weaknesses and frailties as are non-Christian mothers.

If your mother is not a Christian, you may find it easy to idealize what it would be like to have a Christian mom. You might go a step further and blame many normal problems and conflicts on the fact that your mother doesn't know God.

Please keep one thing clearly in mind: It's not your job to cast stones. When you make judgments about your mother, you run the risk of alienating the very person you want to be close to. You may drive a permanent wedge between the two of you.

FIND A CHRISTIAN MOTHER MODEL

Our mothers play an important shaping role in our lives. They train us. They show us how to handle problems, deal with pain, and cope with difficulties. They demonstrate morals and behavior. They reveal to us a philosophy of life.

If your mother is not a Christian, or if she was not a Christian when you were a young child, then she is or was in no position to model Christian living or Christian mothering to you. "I don't know how to show my children what it means to live a Christian life," Peggy said. "It's something I never learned from my mother. I love the Lord, and I tell my children that I do, but in spite of myself, I know I'm inconsistent."

If your mother can't model Christianity to you, you

need to find someone who can. Find an older Christian woman whose life would be an attractive model to you. Spend time with her. See her in action. Ask her questions. Let her fill in the gap left by your non-Christian mom. If you have children, find one or two Christian women who have children the same ages as yours or whose children are just a bit older than yours. Then talk with these women. Tell them about your lack of a godly mother model and ask them to help you be a godly mother. When you have questions about how to handle a certain situation with your children, ask for their advice. Try to be with them when they interact with their children. Find out what their mothers were like.

Don't be ashamed to ask your Christian friends for help and advice. Most will consider it a blessing to be able to help you.

One caution: Don't expect these women to be perfect. They will make mistakes. They will sin. But they still can be models of Christianity in action.

SURRENDER YOUR MOTHER TO GOD

Are you assuming too much responsibility for your mother's spiritual decisions? It's an easy thing to do. It is also a real mistake. All God asks of you is your cooperation. Nothing more. He doesn't ask you to do it all. And he doesn't hold you responsible for what your mom chooses to do with her life. It's appropriate for you to be concerned for her, but if you try to shoulder the Holy Spirit's responsibility to convict her and your mother's responsibility to respond to that conviction, you only hurt yourself—and heap on the guilt.

Consider Jesus' story of the Prodigal Son. We know the dad was grief-stricken over his son's choices, yet we see little of the father's pain and nothing to indicate that he nagged, coerced, pressured, or preached. What we do see is how intently the father watched for his son's return. Finally one day, while his son was still far down the road, the dad spotted him on his way back home. What rejoicing there was! What a celebration!

So it should be between you and your mother. You can pray for her. You can be a witness to her. You can surround yourself with Christians who will support you and advise you. Then you can lovingly turn her over to the Lord.

Of course, not every story ends as happily as the story of the Prodigal Son. Yours may not. But as you wait and pray, keep reminding yourself that God is in control. And you know what? He loves your mother dearly, far more than you ever could. And he is patient, because he doesn't want her to perish (2 Peter 3:9). In the end, however, accepting or rejecting Christ is a choice only your mother can make. It is up to her.

Peggy says that when she finally was able to turn over to the Lord the responsibility of her mother's salvation, when she was finally able to accept the fact that it was her mother's decision to make, not hers, she felt as if a tremendous weight had been lifted from her shoulders. "I've left her in God's hand," Peggy says. "Now I'm going to concentrate on being the loving daughter I'm supposed to be. I'm still praying for her, and I know the Holy Spirit will work in her. But now she's in God's hands, not mine."

What a wonderfully safe and loving place to be!

10.

Making Friends with a Dysfunctional Mother

"Don't talk to me about family life," says Betsy, her voice dripping with bitterness. "All I've ever known from my mom is drunken binges and humiliation. Being raised by an alcoholic mother leaves wounds time can never erase."

"My mother is petite, beautiful, and ever so feminine," says Tiffin-Marie. "My father is tall, burly, and athletic, with a rugged face. Unfortunately, I have more of my father's genes. My mom has never adjusted to having a homely, basketball-playing six-footer for a daughter. She has made little attempt to hide the disappointment and embarrassment I caused her."

When we speak of problems between mothers and daughters, we often think of things like breakdowns in communication or unresolved quarrels or mothers who are too old-fashioned to appreciate their progressive daughters. But many daughters are coping with far more serious problems than these. Many have come from dysfunctional homes, where the problems were so pervasive that just hanging on was a daily struggle. These daughters are trying to make friends with an alcoholic mother or a mother who abused them physically or emotionally or a mother who never protected them from their fathers' abuse, whether it was sexual, physical, or emotional.

DYSFUNCTIONAL MOTHERS

"When my mom would drink, she became violent," Michelle says. "She and my dad would fight and scream at each other. When I would cry during their battles, my mom would tell me, 'All parents fight, Michelle.' So how come nobody else's mother had black eyes or swollen lips or bruised arms?"

Laura's father was a minister, her mom a devoted pastor's wife. "Everyone came to my mom and dad with their problems," she says. "With five kids to raise on a meager income, my parents didn't have much. But my mom liked to say, 'We've always got each other.' Beautiful thought, isn't it? Funny, there was one problem she never bothered to acknowledge—my dad's sexual abuse of me and my sisters. Where was she? Why wouldn't she believe us when we told her he was touching us and asking us to do strange things with him? It's hard to try to make friends with her after all that has happened."

Daughters raised by alcoholic mothers or daughters brought up in abusive homes where they could not depend on their moms to protect and defend them are certainly deeply scarred by their traumatic childhoods. But so are many other daughters raised in less troubled environments.

"She didn't want another child. She made that very clear to me when I was growing up," says Joanne of her mother. "She wanted her career. Her job kept her away from home most of the time. Sometimes I didn't see her for days at a time. My older brothers and sisters watched over me when I was very little, but from the time I was about seven, I pretty much raised myself." Growing up feeling unloved and unwanted is very painful. This kind of emotional abuse can leave a daughter feeling utterly devastated.

Were you raised by a dysfunctional mother? Has your childhood left you feeling inadequate? Do you have deep emotional scars as the result of your mother's behavior?

Well, I have good news for you. You are not helpless. You can make your life different.

TOUGH LOVE

It may be that for years you have hidden your true feelings from your mother, always acting out the part you think she expects of you. Perhaps you have tried repeatedly to win her love and make her proud. Or perhaps you have done your best to shield her from the consequences of her own destructive actions. Maybe you have gone so far as to move your own family way down on your list of priorities so you can run to your mother's side whenever she needs or wants you.

Co-dependence

A subject that has been widely discussed in recent months is co-dependence. If you were raised by a dysfunctional mother, the two of you may have developed a co-dependent relationship. Your mother gets into trouble, you bail her out. She drinks too much, you make excuses for her and drop everything to take care of her until she's better.

Or it may be that the two of you are emotionally co-dependent. Does your mother hold you hostage with her conditional love or threats or bribes? Does she say things like, "If you love me, you'll do this for me"? Does she let you know that you have to do things her way if you expect any love and acceptance from her?

You and your mother have no chance of approaching a healthy relationship until you can remove yourself from your role as her co-dependent. The fact is, you can't be responsible for holding your mother's life together. And you can't continue to fight for her love.

Now that you are an independent adult, you need to set some boundaries. To what degree are you willing to sacrifice your husband or children or close friends for your mother? What are you going to require from your mom? Under what conditions are you willing to come to her assistance? You need to decide on your conditions, then in a kind but firm way let your mother know where you have drawn the lines.

You might say something like, "Mom, I love you, but I have to spend more time with Tom and the children. I want you to call me if you really need me, but I will no longer come over to stay with you when you've been drinking. Or perhaps, "Mom, I love you, and your love is very important to me. But please don't tell me I have to prove my love by taking you places or buying you things. I will do some things for you because I love you. But I want you to understand I love you no less when I have to say no."

After you have drawn your boundary lines, hold to them. If you back down, you've lost. Your mom may threaten, she may push, she may have a temper tantrum or pout or give you the silent treatment. But keep on holding the line. It will be tough. But your determination to stand firm will be the truest demonstration of your love for her.

RISE ABOVE THE PAST

You say your mother will never participate in, accept, or even respond to boundaries you may set? You say there is no way you will ever be able to get through to her? You say her problems go far too deep, that her dysfunctions are too securely rooted for you to ever break through? Then rise above it.

"For years, whenever my alcoholic mother called— which was all the time—I dropped everything to run out to help her," Carolyn said. "As she lay sprawled across her bed, I nursed her and cared for her. When she was feeling better, I cleaned her house, bought some groceries, and cooked up a few dishes to put in her freezer. I didn't leave until I was certain she was all right. That was then. Things are different now."

What made the difference? Carolyn joined Alanon, a support program for families of alcoholics. "I wish my whole family had joined years ago," Carolyn says with a sigh. "Maybe then we really could have helped my mother."

Most daughters raised by alcoholic mothers will need to find outside help. It's not a sign of weakness to realize and admit that handling your mom and her problem is something you can't do alone. Rather, it is a sign of strength. Even if you are not able to get her to ask for help, you can get help for yourself.

BREAK THE MOLD

One of the most pervasive fears shared by daughters of dysfunctional mothers is this: "I'm going to become just like her."

While it's true that your mother has had a great shaping influence on you, it's not true that you are destined to repeat her mistakes. If you don't drink, you will never become an alcoholic. Through counseling and watching other mothers in action, you can unlearn the lessons of abuse your mother taught you and learn to care for your children and to demonstrate your love for them in a consistent and appropriate way.

Are you destined to become a dysfunctional person because of your mother? Not at all! You can choose to be a different person. You may need help from reputable Christian counselors to help heal the wounds and undo the destructive patterns, but you can choose to break the mold. And you can choose to be a better mother. Under your loving training, your daughters probably will be even better mothers to their children than you are to them. What a wonderful legacy to begin and pass along!

PRACTICE FORGIVENESS

For daughters of dysfunctional mothers, the idea of forgiveness takes on a whole new dimension. Instead of dealing with your mother's mistakes in judgment or method, you are dealing with a lifetime pattern of crushing, destructive blows. Whether the blows were physical or emotional or a combination of the two, you surely still bear the scars— perhaps even open wounds—to remind you of what you have endured.

It's important to remember once again that your mother most likely did the best she could under her circumstances. If you think back, you may be able to pick out words or actions that were glimpses of her remorse for what she was doing to you. Try to give her credit for doing the best she could. Remember what we said in chapter 7: Only when you try to understand your mother's background, her circumstances, and her motivations can you begin to move toward forgiveness. With understanding comes forgiveness. With forgiveness comes acceptance. And with acceptance comes love.

You almost certainly will need outside help to enable you to come to the place where you truly can forgive your mother. Again, look for a trusted Christian counselor, preferably one who is skilled in your specific problem area—children of alcoholic mothers, children of physically or emotionally or sexually abusive parents. A counselor who is experienced in marital counseling may not be skilled, for example, in dealing with alcoholism or domestic violence or sexual abuse.

Love your mother, but be willing to put some distance between you. Love her, but determine to rise above the level at which she is existing. Love her, but determine you will not perpetuate her problems. Love her enough to forgive her.

In the New Testament, Jesus says to his followers, "By this all men will know that you are my disciples, if you love one another" (John 13:35). The apostle John adds to this thought later by saying, "Dear children, let us not love with words or tongue but with actions and in truth" (1 John 3:18).

Whatever your mother is, whatever your life together has been like, continue to offer her your love. Love is God's way.

11.

Making Friends with Your Stepmother

Darlene was nine years old when her parents divorced. She and her younger brothers lived with their mother two hundred miles away from their father. When Darlene's dad married Susanna, the new couple determined to gain custody of Darlene and her brothers. "They wanted us to be in a Christian environment," Darlene explains.

Darlene was ten when the four children went to live with her father, stepmother, new stepbrother, and stepsister. "Susanna was nice, but she tried too hard," Darlene says of her stepmother. "She was so strict. No one had ever been strict with us before. And she thought she had all the answers. Whatever I said, whatever I did, she had to have the last word."

Amy was twelve when her mother was killed in a car accident. "I couldn't believe she was gone," Amy says. "She was the one I could always depend on, the one who was always there for me."

One year later, Amy's father remarried. "He thought Norma would be the perfect mother for me," Amy says. "She had six children of her own. But the fact was, she never was that interested in me."

"My mother deserted us when I was in third grade," Kris says. "She was a beautiful woman, tall and elegant. I couldn't believe she cared so little for my brothers and me that she would just walk out and never come back."

It was years before Kris's dad remarried. By then, Kris and her brothers and father, a basketball coach, had carved out a life that suited them fine.

"We lived on canned chili and deli sandwiches, and we spent all our time on the basketball court. It was great. My hair was cut short, and I didn't even own a dress."

Kris's new stepmother was a tall, elegant woman, just like Kris's birth mother. "My stepmother wanted to make a lady out of me too," Kris says with a laugh. "Me! A six-foot tomboy raised on the basketball court by a dad and three older brothers! She sure had her work cut out for her!"

"I was a wife and a mother of two children when my mother died," says Naomi. "My parents had just celebrated their thirty-fifth wedding anniversary. My sister and I showered Dad with love and care even though we lived hundreds of miles from each other. We thought it would take him years to get over his grief—if he ever could. Imagine my horror when he announced a month later that he was going to marry a woman he had met at the bank while settling Mother's affairs!"

Each of these stories is different, and each is very complex. In fact, the issues involved in making friends with your stepmother could fill a book. For our purposes in this chapter we will not discuss Darlene and Kris's need to relate to *both* a stepmother and a birth mother. We will not discuss how the stepdaughter-stepmother relationship is affected by the facts that Darlene had been "taken away" from her birth mother, that Amy's stepmother and six stepchildren had made her feel "shoved out" of the family, that Kris's birth mother had "deserted" her, and that Naomi felt her dad had made a poor decision in marrying her stepmother. And we will not discuss the differences between gaining a stepmother when you were a young girl and gaining one when you are an adult.

What this chapter will explore is how can you make friends with the person whom your dad has chosen to marry—for better or for worse.

STEPMOTHERS

You have to feel sorry for stepmothers. Whatever the circumstances surrounding their introductions into their new families, they start out saddled with a bad reputation. You know the stories: Cinderella, Snow White, Hansel and Gretel. We grew up on storybooks filled with tales of wicked stepmother deeds.

For stepmothers of women like Darlene, it is especially hard. "My mother never met Susanna, but that didn't stop my mom from hating her," Darlene says. "She called her 'the intruder' and the 'husband stealer.' No wonder I had a hard time liking my stepmother."

Too often stepdaughters bring to their stepmothers a background filled with recrimination, resentment, mistrust, and unhappiness. "I didn't care who she was or what she was like," Naomi said. "That woman had known my father only a few weeks. How could she possible love him? I figured she simply caught sight of the size of his estate and latched onto what she saw as a good catch."

Has the wicked stepmother myth become a reality in your family? What are you going to do about it?

Darlene, Amy, Kris, and Naomi want unity and harmony with their stepmothers. They want to make friends with them. If such a friendship is to occur, it will come in three major stages: understanding, acceptance, and affection.

As we have said in earlier chapters, the more you

understand who your mother—in this case, your stepmother—is, the more you will be able to accept her. And the more you can accept her, the closer you will feel to her.

UNDERSTANDING YOUR STEPMOTHER

"Dad would have been fine alone," Naomi says. "He had us. He didn't need a new wife."

Like Naomi, you may find it hard to accept the relationship your father has with his new wife. This change in your family may not be a change you wanted, or one you like.

"It's hard to go visit them," Naomi continues. "I feel like an outsider in the house where I grew up!"

Naomi had no idea what her new stepmother was like. She had no way of understanding the woman's reasons for marrying her dad. It wasn't until Naomi finally allowed herself to learn about her father's new wife's personal and family history that her attitude began to change.

Do you want to become closer to your stepmother? Spend time getting to know her. Ask her about her past experiences. Find out what kind of activities and people she values. Tell each other your life stories.

This kind of sharing may be hard for you to do with your stepmother. You may be reluctant to repeat the special stories your grandparents told you. You may not feel comfortable telling your stepmother funny and embarrassing things from your own childhood.

However, if you really want to make friends with your stepmother, now's the time to try. And now's the time to listen to the stories she has to tell you.

Practice responsive listening with your stepmother. Instead of preparing an answer in your mind while your stepmother is talking and instead of second-guessing what she's going to say, think about what she actually is saying. Try to understand her perspective. Ask her for her opinions. Ask her why she feels the way she does.

And what if your stepmom's comments are critical of you? Let me make a suggestion: Listen to her criticism before you jump in and defend yourself. Consider the possibility, however minute, that her insights just might be accurate. If you think she might have a point, you don't have to say anything right away. Tell her you need to think it over. Ask her, "What would you do if you were in my place?"

Remember, you and your stepmother won't agree on everything. And you don't have to. A few areas of disagreement doesn't mean you can't be friends.

Be willing to be vulnerable. Exposing your own fears and doubts, your own hurts and worries, can go a long way toward breaking down the barriers. Your stepmother probably will trust you a lot more if she sees that you are human too.

If your stepmother responds by sharing some of her own deepest feelings, you might find yourself uncomfortable, maybe even embarrassed. You might not know how to respond. Relax. You needn't be profound. Just say, "I didn't know you felt that way," or "That must be really hard for you." Recognizing her feelings will help you grow closer, even if you don't feel the same way she does.

Don't feel pressured to come up with answers to your stepmother's questions or solutions to her problems. Just allowing her to air her feelings and share her troubles will bring her relief. It's the same for you. Your stepmom probably won't have the answers you are looking for either. Don't expect them. Just appreciate her for being willing to listen.

In trying to understand your stepmother, don't overlook another important resource—your dad. Remember, he's the one who chose to marry her. Ask him about his wife. What qualities in her attracted him? What characteristics does he value in her? Seeing your stepmother through your dad's eyes and through his love and respect for her may help you understand her better.

ACCEPTING YOUR STEPMOTHER

And with understanding comes acceptance. The first step toward accepting your stepmother is realizing you and she are different people with different backgrounds.

"I'd tell her a joke," Amy says of the early days with her stepmother, "and she'd just stand there and look at me. She sure didn't have much of a sense of humor."

"The woman my dad married was a neatness freak," Kris says. "A little mess and clutter didn't bother my brothers and my dad and me at all, but she just about flipped out. She said we lived like four pigs in a pen."

"That first Christmas together was a nightmare," says Darlene. "I never cried so much in my life. Susanna didn't do anything our way. We loved gobs of tinsel on the tree. She said it looked junky and cheap. She had candles burning everywhere. To us our living room looked like a funeral parlor. When Christmas morning came, she made us open our presents one at a time, 'so we can all enjoy them.' We just wanted to rip into our loot!"

Accepting your stepmom is more than gritting your teeth and putting up with your differences. Accepting her involves more than acting politely or nicely toward her. It's more than simply telling her you have accepted her or telling yourself you *have* to accept her. Acceptance requires both time and tolerance.

Time

With time, you can learn to appreciate each other's humor. You can adjust to each other's level of neatness and ideas of politeness. You can develop new holiday traditions. But it takes time. And it takes a willingness to be flexible and to adapt.

Are there things in your stepmother's behavior you find irksome? Think of one specific trait (something that isn't a major character flaw) that drives you up the wall—something like talking too much or chronic lateness. With that trait in mind, ask yourself these questions:

1. Is this quality something I see in myself and don't like?
2. How do I feel when my stepmother does this?
3. Does the behavior remind me of someone from my past?

This exercise can help you focus on the reasons you react negatively to some of your stepmother's behavior. You just may find that understanding and accepting yourself will help you to be less upset by her!

Tolerance

What are your expectations of your stepmother? It may be that you are having trouble accepting her because she doesn't match your image of what she should be. Maybe your imaginary stepmother is quiet and unobtrusive, whereas your real-life stepmother is an absolute talkathon. Maybe your imaginary stepmother is a cuddly, cookie-baking grandma, whereas your real-life stepmother is a well-coifed fashion plate whose main concern about children is that they keep their feet off her white sofa. Accepting your stepmother means folding up that image and putting it away in the attic and getting to know the real person.

Accepting your stepmother also means refusing to compare her to your birth mother. Just because your dad chose to marry your stepmother doesn't mean she will be at all like your birth mother. You do both yourself and your stepmother an injustice if you expect her to be like your birth mother. And your stepmother never will replace your mother. She is a completely different person. As a result, your relationship to her will be very different from your relationship to your birth mother.

SHOWING AFFECTION FOR YOUR STEPMOTHER

As you and your stepmother become more unified through understanding and acceptance, you may find yourselves beginning to feel real affection for each other. The first two stages have laid the groundwork for a caring friendship between you. The more you accept your stepmother, the more you will be able to open up to her. You will lose the fear that she is always watching you, always testing you, always judging you. You will be able to relax more when you're with her, to show her your silly side, to begin to talk about your feelings. Your stepmom will begin to open up around you too. She also will feel more comfortable. No longer will every hug be planned. You may even find that you can get used to those habits that once annoyed you.

As time passes, you will develop a history together, a history made of shared experiences. You both will know the same family dog. You will laugh together over the burned barbecued chicken last Fourth of July. You even will be able to look back at disagreements or problems with a smile:

"Remember how we argued about whose Christmas ornaments to put on the tree? In the end we hung them all. That little tree could hardly stand up under the weight!"

"Remember how I cried the night before your wedding? I was sure if I could get you to call it off, Dad and Mom would get back together. Pretty silly of me, wasn't it?"

Love

If you love your stepmother and she loves you, you can skip over this section. Love becomes a problem only when one of you is looking for it and can't find it. If that's the case with the two of you, let me fill you in on the reality of many stepdaughter-stepmother relationships:

● You are not required to love your stepmom.

- Your stepmother is not required to love you.
- Whatever love does develop between you may come slowly.
- You and your stepmother can be friends even without the kind of love you are worried about not having.

Love takes many forms, portrays many demonstrations, has many meanings. In birth families, love is expected to be unconditional and immediate. In stepfamilies, love grows from understanding, acceptance, and affection. Sometimes your love for your stepmother simply spills over from the great love you feel for your father, who married her. Sometimes your love is expressed simply through your acts of caring.

The loving affection that develops between you and your stepmother doesn't come from the happenstance of birth. It is even better: It is a choice.

When stepdaughters and stepmothers work on their relationship with determination, they often discover they have more resources than they ever realized. Your opportunity for a unique relationship to your stepmother is great because your histories are different, your backgrounds are varied, and you have already met and dealt with so many challenges. With flexibility and imagination, you can build a truly special relationship that is possible between no other two people on this earth.

Your situation most likely is different from Darlene's or Amy's or Kris's or Naomi's. Yet in their stories you may have recognized some elements similar to your own. You may have seen some of your own mistakes—or perhaps some you avoided making. Maybe you felt a twinge of pain or guilt. Maybe you have seen some things you need to stop and consider.

Are you discouraged with the relationship you have been able to form with your stepmother? If so, let me make some suggestions:
- Once you have developed understanding and accept-

ance, look back and see how you've grown. Yes, I mean it. Pretend you're an outsider looking in. Aren't things between you and your stepmother better now than they were? Don't you understand her a little better? Don't you enjoy her a bit more? Appreciate the progress you've made.

● As you consider your relationship, be kind. You are not responsible for the whole thing, you know. You can do only so much. Sure, you may have made some mistakes, but it's not too late to go back and work things out. If you are kinder to yourself, you will find it easier to be kind to your stepmother as well.

● Plan strategies for change and choose among the options available to you. But keep in mind that you are not completely in control of the outcome. If one strategy doesn't work, try another.

● Revise your expectations. Your relationship to your stepmother probably won't fit into that idealistic image you once had. Using those old dreams as a yardstick isn't fair to either of you.

One last thought: Don't give up. If you and your stepmother are working at the understanding level, continue on and be patient. If you have moved to the level of acceptance, good for you. You have a much better relationship in store for you. If you have progressed to the affection stage, congratulations! But don't stop yet. Keep working. The two of you are headed for a true and enduring friendship.

12.

Growing Up Without Wearing Out

Part of a friendship relationship is meeting the other person's needs. That can be a difficult part of a friendship with your mother. Her expectations of your relationship may differ greatly from yours.

Just as daughters may have unrealistic expectations of their moms, many mothers have unrealistic expectations of their daughters as well. Your mother saw your bright baby face and dreamed all kinds of dreams for you. Maybe you've never been able to fulfill those dreams.

"I always thought the relationship between my mom and me was fine," Janelle said. "Then my husband of five years walked out on me. When I called my mom to tell her what had happened, there was just a dead silence. Then, in a cold voice, she said, 'We don't have any divorces in our family.' It was perfectly clear what she was thinking. Her concern wasn't for me. She was worried about what her friends and relatives would think!"

"Even though I never did all that well in school, Mom wanted me to go to college," Meg said. "When I got married halfway through my freshman year, she was so disappointed. Things have never been the same between us since."

"I'm not a musician," Winnie said, "and no amount of piano lessons or hours of practice are going to make me one.

I know how important music is to my mother, and I'm really sorry I've been such a disappointment to her."

"Just once I'd like to talk with my mother without her asking me if I've met any 'nice young men' yet," Kimberly said. "I'd like to sit down with her over a cup of coffee without her whipping out a handful of clippings about biological clocks and children and how much longer married people live than singles. I know she's always wanted me to be married and have a family. But it's my life, and I'm happy just the way it is."

ASSESSING THE EXPECTATIONS

What are the expectations your mother had or has of you? Have you met those expectations? Do you feel inadequate because you have not met some of them? Does she let you know how well you're measuring up?

When considering your mother's expectations for you, you need to ask yourself whether or not they are realistic. Some expectations are appropriate, some are not. If an expectation is appropriate, what can you do to meet it? If it isn't appropriate, how can you let your mother know?

Meredith's seventy-eight-year-old mother, Edith, lives with Meredith. "We do some things together," Meredith says, "but I refuse to entertain her. When she first came to live with me, that's what she expected. But being together all the time wasn't good for either of us."

With Meredith's help, Edith has established for herself a nice network of friends and activities. She plays the piano at church and participates in their weekly senior-citizens' group meetings. Once a month she goes on a tour with her church group. She enjoys being involved in the community, and every Thursday she volunteers in the local hospital's children's playroom. Through church and the hospital, Edith has made a number of new friends with whom she visits, goes for walks, and has lunch.

"I owe Meredith a lot of credit," Edith says. "I came

here thinking she should be my constant companion. Instead, she helped me find my place in this new city. Once I got established, she encouraged me to lead my own life. Oh, yes, we see each other all the time. But she insisted my life should be mine and her life should be hers. She was right."

HANDLING UNREALISTIC EXPECTATIONS

Meredith understood exactly what her mother expected of her. But she also knew that expectation was unrealistic—for both of them.

It's important that you understand what your mother expects of you. Not understanding her expectations may lead to real frustration. Only when you do understand her expectations can you begin to deal constructively with them.

Be Kind

Although it may be obvious to you that what your mother expects of you is totally unrealistic, in her mind it isn't unrealistic at all.

"I want Kimberly to find a nice young man, get married, and have children because I know in the long run that's what will make her happy. She likes her job, but what about when she gets to be my age? She won't have that job, and all those friends will be gone. She'll be alone and unhappy, and it will be too late to do anything about it. I only want what's best for my daughter."

It's true. She does. That's how mothers are. If Kimberly were to respond by telling her mother to mind her own business and quit interfering, it could be devastating to her mother.

It is possible to be both kind and firm. For instance, Kimberly could say brightly, "So far I haven't met the right man. Maybe I will some day. But even if I don't, I feel that my life is fulfilling. I would rather be single and feel I'm doing the right thing than marry the wrong person. I'm satisfied with my life, Mom, and I hope you can come to the point where you are satisfied with it too."

Don't Reject Your Mother

You can let your mother know you consider her expectations unrealistic without rejecting her. Resist saying things like, "You're living in the past. You don't know what life is all about nowadays," or "Music, music, music! Your whole life is music!"

Set a Logical Course for Redesigning Her Expectations

Meredith could have told her mother, "I can't spend all my time with you. I have a life of my own!" Instead, she helped her mother redesign her expectations and get established in a circle of friends and activities she could really enjoy.

Realistic Expectations Can Work for Both of You

When Lynda's mother, Dorothy, came to live next door to Lynda and her family almost five years ago, she expected to spend some time each day with Lynda's family. Lynda saw it differently.

"I keep trying to introduce her to people her age and to get her involved in interesting groups," Lynda says. "There's a real good group for senior citizens in our church, but the few times I've managed to drag Mom out to it, she's acted bored and not the least bit interested in meeting anyone. I don't know what else I can do. I just want her to be happy!"

Lynda's expectations are frustrating to her mother. "I'm not a helpless old woman," Dorothy insists. "And I'm not Lynda. She likes to be in the thick of things. She likes people around her, and she always wants to be going places and doing things. Not me. I like to sit at home by the fire and read and sew. I like sleeping late in the morning and working in my garden and taking walks in the evening. I like to visit with my family. Just because it's not her idea of fun doesn't mean I'm not happy."

With a sigh Lynda says, "I wish I could get mom to understand that the reason I prod her and encourage her to make changes is because I care about her."

Both Lynda and her mother need to sit down and talk over the situation in a loving, sensitive way. Both are doing what they think is best. But neither is listening to the other.

WHAT IF YOUR MOTHER EXPECTS THE IMPOSSIBLE FROM YOU?

You can't do the impossible. You owe it to yourself and to your mother to decide just what you will and what you will not do for her. Tell her where you can meet her expectations and where you can't.

To make this determination, you must consider the other demands on your life. Do you have a husband and children? They need your time too. Do you have a job? Do you have outside interests? Although your mother is important to you, you need to consider her needs in the context of the other demands on your time and energy.

Once you have made your decision, talk it over with your mother. Tell her your thoughts, and let her know you are ready and willing to listen to hers.

If your mother tends to be overdependent on you, help her to see the area for which she must take responsibility. But don't just leave it there. Be ready to suggest specific ways your mother can meet her own needs.

WHEN YOUR MOTHER'S HEALTH IS POOR

If your mother is older or in poor health, you'll have an added problem. It may be difficult to know whether you are responding to her with appropriate concern and compassion or with inappropriate guilt and responses you thought you had outgrown long ago.

You love your mother. The two of you have a long and intense history together. Certainly if you react to her pain by giving her sympathetic support and if you do whatever you can to alleviate her discomfort, that is an appropriately kind and loving response.

But some mothers' pain and suffering may be imagined rather than real. "Every time my husband and I want to go off together for the weekend, my mother gets heart palpitations," Claire says. "I can't leave her when she's sick. If anything was to happen, I'd never forgive myself."

Some mothers have a chronic way of provoking their daughters into doing what they want. Claire's mother knew how to keep her daughter at home where she wanted her. It worked every time.

The appropriate response to your mother's pain and suffering depends on its source and purpose. When she is not accusing you of causing her suffering or of failing to rescue her from it, you should respond with loving compassion. But when pain and suffering are her usual ways of getting you to do what she wants you to do, you are responding to her out of guilt. That is not appropriate.

WHEN YOUR MOTHER ACTS LIKE A CHILD

It may be that at some point you will come to the exasperated realization that your mother is acting more like a spoiled, obstinate child than like a rational adult. Raising a young child is not like raising the "child" in your mother. A young child's dependency is more appropriate to her age. A young child has real needs that must be met before she can move on to the next stage. Your mother's dependency, on the other hand, may not be appropriate to her age. Her expectations may be totally unreasonable.

Your mother's childishness may be the result of the

way she herself was mothered. Her needs may not have been met when she was a child. But no matter what you do, you can never make up for what she didn't get. Trying to satisfy the child needs in her is futile. To persist in trying will only result in frustration, despair, and an incredible emotional drain on you.

Give up the illusion of fulfilling these unrealistic needs in your mother. Help her to recognize her needs for what they are, but insist that she take responsibility for getting those needs met in appropriate ways.

Make sure that you grow up without wearing out. Determine which of your mother's expectations you will try to meet and which you can't meet. Then let your mother know where you stand. Let her know that you feel her needs are important but that you are not the person to meet all of them. Discuss how she might be able to meet some of her needs, but leave the responsibility with her.

Encourage your mom to accept the responsibility for her own happiness. Free yourself from crippling guilt. You have a right to look your relationship straight in the eye and say, "This is not acceptable." The belief that just because your mother has a need, you are obligated to meet that need is a myth. In feeling free to say no to your mother's manipulative pressure, you will free yourself to grow. What's more, you most likely will enable your mother to grow as well.

13.

Full Circle: Mothering Your Mother

It's hard to identify the exact moment when a mother becomes the child and her child becomes the mother. I guess it's a lot of firsts lumped together: The first time you zip your mother's dress because she can't get her arms over her shoulders. The first time she asks you to thread her needle because she can't find the glasses hanging around her neck from a chain. The first time you step in and rescue her because she can't remember the name of the woman who has lived next door for twenty years.

With an eerie shiver you suddenly realize this is the person who used to dress you when you couldn't make the buttons and buttonholes come out even. It was she who taught you to thread a needle. She was the one who used to rescue you from all the adults who looked alike by saying, "Dear, you remember Mrs. Jameson, don't you?"

Suddenly everything is turned around. Your roles have become reversed. If you had thought about it, you would have known this was likely to happen sometime. But it's the kind of thing we all figure happens only to other people. What a shock it is to see those first signs of dependency becoming evident in your very own mother.

AGING AMERICA

America is aging. The top family issue of the 1980s was child care. But now, and continuing on and into the next century, the critical issue is the care of the elderly. Statistics tell us that women are much more likely than men to be the ones who will bear the brunt of caring for both children and elderly parents.

Are you ready for a really sobering thought? Statistics also indicate that most of us will spend more years caring for our aging parents than in rearing our own children. According to professionals, on the average, women spend seventeen years of their lives taking care of their children and eighteen years assisting their aging parents.

Remember all the talk about the empty-nest syndrome—that emotional vacuum many women experience when their grown children leave home? For many of us, it may be short-lived. That "nest" will likely be re-filled with frail parents, parents-in-law, or other relatives.

For the so-called "baby bust" generation that follows the much-discussed "baby boomers," the problem is even greater. For the first time in history, we have a generation of American couples who have more parents than they have children.

Today, a woman whose children are grown has completed, on the average, less than half the caregiving she will provide during her lifetime. Many of us see no empty nest in sight. Far from being free of responsibility when our children get out on their own, our most difficult years will still be ahead.

Extra years together—a blessing or a curse? For mothers and daughters who have achieved a true friendship, it can be a wonderful blessing. For those who are struggling with resentments and bitterness and anger, it can be a thing to dread.

MOTHERING YOUR MOTHER

Even though you know that such a reversal of your parent-child roles is possible—even likely—when it actually comes, it will probably still hit you hard. For as you have seen, you often relate to your mother as your parent, and she continues to regard you as her child. Then suddenly you find your mother depending on you for help with remembering things, for making decisions, and for physical things like getting to the doctor, driving to the shopping center, reading the fine print on the pill bottle—the kinds of things she did as a mother.

You may be genuinely glad to be able to help your mother when she needs you. But don't be surprised if you still feel a very real sense of loss. No longer can you comfort yourself with the belief—even if it was no more than a wishful hope—that come what may, you could always turn to your mother, that she would always be there for you.

Now, I'm not suggesting your sense of responsibility come from a feeling of obligation simply because society or your church or your own guilt says you should take care of your mother. I hope that it will come more from a genuine sense of commitment to care for a person who has been very important to you. She certainly has an authentic claim to your loving attention. And if your relationship to your mother has blossomed into one of friendship, she will have an extra-special claim. She needs your help, comfort, advice, and support—all qualities of friendship.

"My active, beautiful, society mother had a sudden heart attack, followed by bypass surgery," said Leslie. "The doctor warned us her struggle back to health would be slow and painful. My seventy-one-year-old dad had never done any housekeeping or caregiving in his life, so my husband and I moved in to care for both of them.

"I should admit right up front that my mother and I have always had a stormy relationship. Mom was a glossy-type person, an actress and a model. I graduated in the seventies, a full-blown hippie who rejected all the trappings of materialism. I was super critical of my mother and all she stood for. And she was obviously disappointed in me. Never did she let up on her pressure for me to be successful by her definition. Never did she quit hoping I would suddenly turn into a glamorous model.

"When she got sick, a surprising thing happened. All her glamor suddenly dropped away. For the first time in my life I got a glimpse of what my unadorned mother was like. And for the first time I saw her helpless and vulnerable, the very way I had so often felt in her presence. Suddenly I was all decked out, giving Mom massages and cooking special dishes for her, and she was the crumpled, frightened, insecure person."

The role reversal may feel good at first. "Mom always had been such a martyr," Leslie continued. "At home she did everything. I couldn't do anything well enough to suit her. Suddenly she was in a place where she had to accept my help. It was good for both of us."

But as time goes on, we may begin to chafe under the unfamiliar role and the new responsibilities. As with Leslie, the change may occur when you are at a stage in life when your marriage, your children, your career, or your desire for independence is your highest priority.

CAUGHT IN THE MIDDLE

Daughters in Leslie's situation often find themselves caught between the demands of their teenage or young adult children and those of their aging parents. Nearly two million women already fit into this so-called "sandwich generation" who are caring simultaneously for both their children and their parents. And the number is growing each year. One exasperated mother said, "My advice to my seventy-two-year-old mother is the same as to my seventeen-year-old daughter. To both of them I say, 'For goodness' sake, act your age!'"

When you find yourself pressured from both sides, both emotionally and financially, ask yourself this question: Whose needs should take precedence? If your mother truly needs your assistance, you may find yourself confronted with a serious dilemma. It might help to put it to yourself this way: "I know my mother's needs are legitimate. What, then, am I willing—and able—to do to help her deal with those needs?"

Too many adult daughters make decisions that affect their aging mothers without ever bothering to consult them. Unless your mother is truly incompetent, talk with her about the options. Share your thoughts and concerns with her. Listen to her thoughts and concerns too. Ask if she has any other ideas. If at all possible, let your mother make the final decision.

DEVELOP REALISTIC EXPECTATIONS

Perhaps the key to dealing effectively with the challenges of an aging parent is to have realistic expectations. Go ahead and take on those things you *can* do for her, but don't punish yourself for those things you can't do. Remember, you can't change who your mother is, and you can't do too much about how she reacts to your help.

One thing you can do, however, is find out if any of her physical and emotional symptoms can be treated. It may be that your mother's physical complaints, failing memory, confusion, and insomnia can be treated. What seems to you to be senility or hopeless signs of old age actually may be symptoms of something treatable such as depression, diabetes, or a hearing loss.

Another thing you can do is to continue treating her as a friend you love and respect. Every aging mother presents different challenges and responds in different ways. Be patient as your mother-friend struggles to meet her own challenges and to find her own ways of responding.

A third contribution you can make to your mother's life is to encourage her to be as independent as she is physically and mentally able to be. By treating your mother as if she were a child or an invalid, you will be taking away too much of her dignity, her spirit, and her will to live and be productive.

As long as your mom has strong legs, let her walk. As long as she has hands, let her do. As long as she has a mind, let her make decisions. As long as she has ideas, let her talk about them. As long as she has opinions, let her share them. As long as she has a purpose in life, let her pursue and enjoy it. As long as she lives, treat her as a friend.

As your mother ages, you may find yourself aching to step in and take care of her. Not only will you zip her dress for her, but you will get her coat, help her into it and button it up. When she asks you to thread her needle, you will insist on sewing in her hem. When she forgets her neighbor's name, you will take it as a sign of her inability to control her life and you'll take over.

Remember your own struggle for independence? Remember how you bristled when your mother wanted to do for you what you could very well do for yourself? Remember how you hated it when she always thought she knew what was best for you? Whenever you are tempted to take over for your mother, remember: You need your independence, and so does she.

The time may come when it is no longer possible for your mother to be independent. If she can't drive safely, she ought not to be driving. If she can't live alone without undue risk, other living arrangements will have to be made. You may be able to make a home for your mother with your family, or you may not. Look into the options available. Is there another family member more suited to having her? Is there a good senior residence or nursing home near you? If your mother is able, include her in the decision-making. Let her know the options available to her. And as much as possible, let the final decision be hers.

THE STRONGEST FRIENDSHIP OF ALL

Certainly your mother's aging will present you with physical and emotional challenges. But it can also give you something else: special opportunities to build a stronger bond of intimacy and trust between you. Perhaps now you finally will have a chance to find out more about her childhood. Ask her about her memories of significant historical events that occurred during her lifetime. Go through her old photographs and ask her about the people in them. As you listen to her stories about Grandmother Edith and Granduncle Dewey, you may want to make some notes, maybe even turn on a tape recorder, so her memories won't be lost to future generations.

Ask your mother about your first years of life. You probably will find her stories of joys and heartaches and the insights she has gained through them not only moving but also extremely helpful. Sorting through old photos, recalling people and events from the past, learning more about what made your mom who she is and you who you are, can be a rewarding experience indeed—for both of you. Through it you may end up closer than ever.

THE FINAL STAGE

For many of us, our most difficult challenge of all will come during the months or years after our mothers are found to have a terminal illness. The hardest thing in the world is to live with uncertainty. If you find yourself in this situation, you probably will cry out in desperation, "I've got to *do* something!" only to find there's nothing to be done. As you stand helplessly by, you may be surprised at the feelings of guilt that surge forward. Over and over you may find yourself repeating, "If only I had (or hadn't) . . ."

And there's more. Not only will you have to deal with your own inner turmoil, but you probably will feel the burden of dealing with your mother's needs as well.

Many daughters of aging or dying parents are uncertain how, or even if, they should express their own ideas and opinions. They don't want to say the wrong thing and maybe end up getting caught in an argument. The important thing is to consider your mother's needs and feelings. From that base point, see if you can find a way to express your own viewpoints and ideas without seeming to be critical or trying to change her. If you have already learned to communicate with your mother, this stage will be easier for both of you.

Remember, whenever possible, let your mom make the choices in matters that will affect her. State your opinion and the reasons for it, then say, "Here are your options, Mom. It's up to you. Whatever you decide, I'll support you. My main concern is that you be comfortable and that you know I'm with you whatever happens."

And you know what? Dying does not have to be a terrible thing. Especially not for the person who truly believes that when Christians die, they are "away from the body [but] at home with the Lord" (2 Cor. 5:8).

Lovingly sharing and communicating at the end of her life can give both you and your mother a final chance to heal any residual wounds in your relationship. By using your last little while this way, you may be spared the empty feeling of being left with unfinished business, unspoken love, and the guilt and remorse so many daughters experience. If your fences have already been mended, it will give you one final opportunity to seal your friendship.

Unfinished Business

"For months after my mother died," Mary Jo said, "I had the same dream. Night after night I would be running down a dark hall begging her to talk to me. I'd promise to listen to her stories. I'd beg her to let me sit by her and hear her sing 'Rock of Ages.' Then I'd awaken to the realization that my mother was gone. It was too late for me to give her the time she had so longed for in life."

Each of us, to a greater or lesser degree, feels guilty when our mother dies. Working through that guilt and all our regrets requires letting go of those "if onlys." They merely prevent us from making peace with our mother.

Don't leave unfinished business. If your mother is still alive, do and say the important things now. Spend time with her. Tell her that you love her. Tell her what you appreciate about her.

However, if your mother has already died and it's too late to do and say those things, it may help to sit down and write your mother a letter. In it you can list all those regrets you feel about your relationship to her, all the things you wish you hadn't done—or that you didn't do and wish you had. Include everything you long to have told her while she was alive. It may be that these memories will come easily. Sometimes they do. If not—if your regrets are too deeply submerged—it might help to write out several different letters. Even though she can no longer read it, it will do you good to express your thoughts.

Acceptance

To accept your mother's death means to be at peace with both the happy and the sad times you shared, with the parenting and the battling and the friendship. And understanding the impact both your mother's life and her death had on you may include discovering how your conflicts and difficult times helped you to become a stronger and more capable person, maybe even a better mother. And it will help you understand how the friendship that grew between the two of you formed the special relationship you shared. This, too, might help you be a better mother, one who knows how to be a friend to her children.

Some daughters, when they think of their mothers, remember only the fights and the anger and the bitterness. Others block everything from their memories but the good times. Making peace with your mother allows you to benefit from all the experiences in your relationship—including the most rewarding friendship of your life—and to grow as a result of every one of them.

14.

Bylaws for Daughters

One of the purposes of this book is to bridge the so-called generation gap with a bond of loving friendship. If the gap is so wide and so securely in place that it is too difficult to span just yet, our goal is to narrow the gap and aim to prevent the gap from growing into a chasm.

You can build bridges. No matter who and what you are. No matter who and what your mother is. Whether she is loving or cold, cooperative or stubborn, a close friend or a distant one. Whether she is a demonstrative communicator or quiet and reserved. Whether you and she are alike or absolute opposites. Bridges can be built. And it is up to you to oversee their construction.

As you reach out with greater understanding toward your mother, you will recognize that she is struggling to find a new place and function in life, that she is laboring to establish herself in a rapidly changing, more uncertain world than the one in which she learned the rules of life. In the process you probably will find her drawing closer to you. The result will be a truer mutual understanding between you. With this accomplished, you and your mom will have laid the foundation stones for a bridge of enduring friendship.

In this book you have read a lot of suggestions, ideas, and guidelines. They can be summarized into a list of bylaws for daughters. If you truly want to build or improve a successful lifelong friendship with your mother, you might want to review these bylaws and make them part of your life.

Define Your Relationship

At what stage is your relationship with your mother now? Unless you know where you are starting from, how will you know where you are going? And how will you know when you get there? Think about what your relationship is now, and decide how you would like to see it change.

Admit Your Mom Isn't Perfect

This is a good starting point. Your mom isn't perfect. But then, no person on earth is. Expecting her to be perfect puts her under a crushingly unfair burden. Learn to accept her faults and maximize her strengths.

Learn to Communicate

Don't talk *at* your mom. Don't even talk *to* her. Talk *with* her. There's a huge difference, you know. No matter how old your mother is, no matter how unreasonable you find her to be, no matter how hard you may have to struggle to get through to her, let your conversations be two-sided— thoughtful sharing and responsive listening. When she is talking, try to listen for what is behind the words, to her feelings or to the experiences from which her words come. That's what communication is all about.

Share Perspectives

If your mother does something that bothers you a little, overlook it. If she does something that bothers you a lot, talk with her about it. Nothing can be gained by stewing in silence. Give your mother a chance to see the matter from your perspective. And give her the opportunity to help you see it from hers. If she changes sides, the problem is solved. If you find her side is not all that bad after all, you can surely learn to live with it. If she refuses to change and if what she's doing still drives you crazy, at least you both know where the other stands.

Share Expectations

Understand your mother's expectations of you. Understand your expectations of her. Which expectations are realistic? Which are not? After you have done some examining, be ready to do some adjusting.

Get to Know Your Mother

I mean *really* get to know her. What were her parents like? Where was she raised? How was her background different from yours? What is her motivation for doing the things she does and for saying the things she says? In what ways are you alike? In what ways are you different?

Accept Your Differences

Recognize that there are going to be differences between you and your mother. You're not the same person she is. That's all right. And remember, your mom is entitled to her own opinions. Accept the fact that you don't have to agree on everything in order to be friends. And as with any other friend, be willing to overlook and adapt.

Find Out What Is Important to Your Mom

Take the time and trouble to find out what is important to your mother. If you don't, how can you really talk with her? You can't expect her to be engrossed in your life and your interests when you care little about hers.

Include Your Mother

Find the time to include your mother in some of the things you and your family do. I know, I know. She may not fit in with your friends or many of your activities. Or she may end up just complaining. Or if you include her a little, she may expect to become a permanent part of everything you do.

The point here is for you to remain in control. Include her regularly, always being as positive as you possibly can, then when it's an occasion in which you do not wish to include her, be firm. You might say, "No, Mom, I didn't invite you to my dinner party. I can seat only ten around my table. But the whole family is certainly looking forward to our picnic on Saturday. I'm making that potato salad you like so much."

Allow Your Mom Time Alone

On the other hand, don't try to force your mother to spend all her time with you. She is perfectly capable of arranging her own time to be alone, to be with friends, or to do activities she enjoys. Just because she doesn't choose to be with you frequently doesn't mean she doesn't love you. And allowing her time alone does not suggest you are a neglectful daughter. It just means she needs some time away from you.

Give Her the Benefit of the Doubt

Maybe your mother is the type that is always giving you advice. Sometimes it may be the same old thing again, but it just may be that she really has something worth sharing with you. Your mother does have experience in living and parenting, you know. And she just may have a good deal more wisdom and insight than you realize. As one mother said, "You don't know what it's like to be my age. But I know exactly what it's like to be yours."

Learn to Handle Conflict, Anger, and Criticism

At one time or another, if your relationship with your mother is long enough and close enough, you will experience conflict. You may feel anger between you. Your mother may criticize you. Knowing these emotions are likely to come up, you can think ahead about how you will handle them. You might even want to go so far as to compose specific comments and examples to use.

Refuse to Be Manipulated

Manipulation is a choice. Your mother can't manipulate you if you refuse to be manipulated. It's up to you. If you decide to allow yourself to be used, don't complain that your mother is using it against you.

Give Your Relationship a High Priority

Let your mom know your relationship is really important to you. If the going gets tough, refuse to give up. Keep on working to develop your friendship relationship, and keep expecting positive results.

Take the Initiative

If you just wait for your relationship to improve, it probably never will. If you wait for your mother to change, it probably won't ever happen. If you truly want a new, improved, healthy friendship with your mother, you will have to take the initiative. You will have to make it happen.

Respect Your Mother's Privacy

Understand that you are not entitled to know everything about your mother's life. She is also an adult, and she has been one much longer than you have. And make it a rule not to drop in on her unexpectedly. Let her know you respect her privacy. It may be a real temptation to "just stop by," but you probably will be more welcome if you call first and ask if it's convenient.

Unless her condition requires it, don't telephone her every day just to check up on her. Don't always ask her where she's going and with whom or where she's been. She's been an adult for a long time. She probably will resent it if you try to control her life at this stage.

Develop Friendships and Hobbies

You and your mom are not attached at the hip. And you are not responsible for entertaining each other or keeping each other happy. It's up to each of you to make your own happiness.

Be Patient

Don't expect overnight changes. Your mom's behavior and pattern of reactions are deeply ingrained in her (just as yours are). She has been rehearsing and perfecting them over the years (just as you have). If you start out expecting the process of change to take time, you won't be so easily discouraged.

Don't Be Quick to Correct

Be careful not to correct your mother constantly. So what if she is mistaken? So what if she's wrong? Most of the time it makes no difference at all. Don't expect or demand perfection from her, and maybe she will allow you the same space. Remember, you aren't raising a child. You are dealing with a full-fledged adult. Be content to love her and enjoy her company.

Watch that you don't criticize her in front of her friends. That can be a humiliating experience for her. Neither she nor they are likely to appreciate your interference. If your mother wants your help or advice, she will surely ask for it.

Help Your Mom Stay Independent

Whenever possible, let your mom lead her life without too much interference from you. She will be much happier to have you around when she wants or needs you. By making your mother dependent before it is absolutely necessary, you will be doing no one a favor, especially not her. Even though it may take time and patience on your part, give her the dignity of doing for herself just as long as she can.

Affirm Your Mother

Affirm your mom whenever she acts in ways that deepen your friendship. Most likely, building a better relationship was your idea. She may think things are just fine the way they are. When you recognize gestures that show she appreciates your relationship, give her a hug and tell her how much you appreciate her.

Compliment Your Mother

Compliment her often. Say "thank you" when thanks are due. It's too easy to assume that a kind deed or a thoughtful gesture required little time and almost no effort on her part. Whether your assumption is right or wrong, your mother will appreciate having you express your gratitude. "I love you" and "You mean so much to me" and

"I know we see things differently, and I do so appreciate the way you listen to and respect my opinions" are powerfully effective phrases. Pepper your conversation with these kinds of statements and you'll be positively surprised with the response you get.

Mothers and daughters have the potential for the most precious, most enduring, and most satisfying of relationships. But it isn't something that just happens. It takes awareness, and it takes effort. It takes understanding. It takes faith and trust. And it takes love and patience.

But making friends with your mother is worth the effort!